The Illustrated Art Of
Teaching Soccer
To Your Children

By Bob Swope
1st Edition 2004

Published and distributed by:
Jacobob Press LTD.
St. Louis, Mo.
(314) 843-4829, E-Mail: jacobobsw@msn.com

ISBN: 0-9705827-3-0

Printed and Bound by:
Hardbound, Inc.
St. Louis, MO 63045

First Edition 2004

This book is dedicated to three of my favorite soccer players. My grandchildren. Who are playing now, or have played a lot of soccer games over the years. I hope they can find some techniques or tactics in this book that will help them improve on their skills.

PAUL

CATHERINE

ZEPHERIN

AUTHORS ACKNOWLEDGMENT

My thanks to the 2003 and 2004 edition 4th grade girls and boys soccer teams, and their coach's from St. Catherine Laboure Parish in St. Louis, Mo. for all their help in putting together the pictures for this book. The pictures will really help illustrate what I am trying to get across to everyone using this book, and that is to help children improve on their soccer skills.

GIRLS TEAM

BOYS TEAM

ABOUT THE AUTHOR

Bob Swope, is a long time youth sports coach, teacher, and author. He has 17 years experience coaching and teaching kids, both boys and girls. His teams are known for their knowledge and use of the fundamentals. His philosophy is kids will have more fun out there when they know the basic fundamentals, and how to apply them. He has taken a team of left over kids, after a draft was performed, and taken them to a championship and playoffs in just three years. This was basically accomplished just by teaching them the fundamentals, and getting good knowledgeable coaches to work on these fundamentals every day with the kids. He has coached and managed in four different sports. He has taken a lot of training and teaching techniques from one sport and used them in another. He has been a member of the "Youth Football Coaches Association of America", and is currently working with the "National Youth Sports Coaches Association" to get certification in several sports.

TABLE OF CONTENTS

1. **Introduction**..6

2. **Attitude Developers**..8
   - *Influence*...8
   - *Their Improving* 8
   - *Respect* 9
   - *Hustle* 10
   - *Health Habits* 10

3. **The Fundamentals**..11
   - *What are They*..11
   - *Forwards, Strikers, and Wingbacks* 12
   - *Midfielders, Left and Right Midfielders*.................13
   - *Defenders, Center Backs, and Fullbacks* 13
   - *Sweepers*...14
   - *Goalkeepers* 15

4. **Organize your Teaching**...15

5. **Drills and Exercises** 16
   - *How do they help*...16
   - *Warm up and Stretching* 16
   - *Coordination and Agility* 21
   - *Controlled Falling & Field Presence*......................24
   - *Strength* 27
   - *Cool downs* 32
   - *Dribbling* 32
   - *Passing* 38
   - *Ball Feel & Control* 50
   - *Trapping and Receiving* 56
   - *Throwing* 60
   - *Heading* 64
   - *Tackling* 64
   - *Blocking & Stealing*..72

Faking & Tricking...73

Protecting the Ball 82

Running, Quickness & Endurance 83

Chipping and Volleying 88

Kicking & Shooting Goals.................................91

Goalkeeping..101

The Kickoff 116

Defending and Marking...................................119

6. Formations 122

7. New Parent Orientation 124

Offensive Game 125

Defensive Game 127

8. The Playing Field 129

9. General Game Rules 131

10. Referee's & Penalties 134

11. Soccer Terminology............................141

12. Equipment 147

13. Other Available Books.......................152

14. Index..154

*******WARNING*******

If your child or the participant has any physically limiting condition, bleeding disorder, high blood pressure, pregnancy or any other condition that may limit them physically you should check with your doctor before participating in these drills and exercises.

Be sure participants, making hard contact, are of the same weight and size to avoid injury.

All Drills and exercises should be supervised by an adult. **AUTHOR ASSUMES NO LIABILITY FOR ANY ACCIDENTAL INJURY OR EVEN DEATH THAT MAY RESULT.**

EXTRA CARE AND CAUTION SHOULD BE TAKEN WITH ANY OF THE TACKLING AND HEADING EXERCISES, AS THEY ARE THE MORE DANGEROUS ONES.

Introduction

My personal envolvement with teaching soccer started in just the last year or so. However I have been following soccer in the St. Louis area since the 1982 season, with the old "St. Steamers" MISL indoor soccer team. I know there is a lot of differences between the outdoor game, and the indoor game. But most of the basic fundamentals, for young kids to learn, are the same. And these are what I am going to focus on. Most of my experience has been working with local "CYC" coaches, and teams. Since this book is for young boys, and girls, in the 5 to 12 year old range, their next step from youth sports will be to high school athletics. What I will be illustrating is what high school coaches would like the kids to already basically know when they get there. Recently the experts have studied many of the old standard conditioning exercises in youth sports, and they came up with better ways to accomplish the same thing. So what you are reading in this book is some of the latest information on how to teach kids stretching, strengthening, and endurance exercises, with less chance of them getting an injury.

The idea of a soccer reference book for young boys has that certain appeal for me because when I was at this age there were no books out there for my dad to refer to, so he could help me learn about a sport. He was not into athletics much, since he came from an era when men started to work at a young age, and I guess he never thought about sports. So this book is dedicated to all those mothers and fathers who would like their children to be the best they can be, and also have some fun while learning.

Usually mom and dad would like to see them get outside more, and get involved in sports for the exercise, but they probably don't know what sport to get them into. Well maybe soccer is the sport. Most kids naturally like to run and kick large beach type balls around. The boy or girl that more than likely doesn't want to play youth baseball, basketball, or football, might be just be afraid they don't have the skills to play those sports. Or you may just have a boy, or girl, that does not like those sports. And some of you single moms, maybe you have a son or daughter that you would like to get out there and do something with. But maybe you just don't know how to go about it. All of you that are in this situation can use this book to help them learn more about how to get ready to play soccer. The average mom and dad don't know what they can do to have some fun with their son or daughter, and also teach them something about soccer while doing it. Well for all of you out there, here is a book you can use as a guide or reference manual with pictures. Take it with you out to the yard, and use it as you go about teaching and having some fun.

As a member of the "Youth Football Coaches Association of America", I was sent to coaching clinics to learn coaching techniques, and how to treat injuries. I have been interested for a long time in conditioning for sports. Due to careful team training, other than minor bumps and bruises, I can only remember two injuries on teams I have been directly connected with. And this was over a six year period. One boy had bruised ribs, and my oldest son had a broken wrist. This would be only two injuries out of a possible 1380 boys playing, over a six year span. It's not perfect, but I am proud of this record.

No book can not turn a boy or girl into a STAR player in a sport, if they do not have at least some talent. I can't think of any book that could do that. However this book will help them to improve their basic soccer skills, and grow up to be a better person, and a team player in life. And also it will be a lot of fun for you to get out and work with your son or daughter. I can recall that these were some of the best times of my life. My sons and I still talk about them when we get together. Soccer will also teach them how to work with other people as a team. And it follows that the game will be more fun for them as they learn more about the basic fundamentals. They will feel good because their knowledge of soccer will impress all of their friends. All the hours of practice might also keep them out of trouble as long as you don't over do it because they won't have a lot of free time to get into trouble. Another thing that will help them is some youth soccer leagues they join, might have a policy that they keep their grades up in school while playing. And this is very important as they go into the higher grades in school. When you stop and think about it you, and your son or daughter *working together,* could become a turning point in both of your lives in many ways.

Attitude & Behavior Development

Influence

Boys from the age of *five through eight* are very impressionable, and mom and dads influence can be important in their development at this stage of learning. It is also important to teach young boys, and girls that youth soccer is only a game, and what is most important for them to realize is to develop good sportsmanship. Explain that they should always try their best, and if they don't do well every time there is always another day. One of the things I have learned is that if something is worth doing, then try to be the best you can be at it. I realize this is very hard for some young kids to learn. So, what I always told the kids, on my teams, was have someone watch you to see what it is you might be doing wrong. Then that person should work with them, over and over, to correct these things. I explained to them that if they worked hard, they would begin to see that they were getting better and better. If your son or daughter has a good attitude then this will usually be reflected to the rest of the kids on the team. In other words it can be contagious, to everyone else on the team.

Their Improving

Part of improving their attitude towards other players on the team, coaches, managers, and referees, will depend a lot on how YOU normally act. Your son or daughter will most often reflect your attitude towards these people. So, be very aware of what you say when they are present, or nearby. Many times I have seen parents screaming from the sidelines at referees, or another kid on the team, when they think they have made a mistake. Then, following your example, during practice, your son or daughter will belittle one of their team mates or the coach. This is really just learned behavior from YOU. And as parents we have to be honest with ourselves, we are not perfect, so why should we expect everyone else to be. Think about it, if a team has to rely on a referee's call, or a team being perfect to win the game, then maybe they didn't deserve to win. A parents bad attitude just makes things worse not better. My advice to you is just bite your tongue so to speak, until you cool off a bit, and you find that you will have a lot more fun out there.

So please instruct him or her to get along with their team mates. Because if they are a better player than their team mates, they can help them more by encouraging them than by belittling them. It will help in showing their team mates how they can become a better player, like your son or daughter is. This way the whole team gets better. And when that happens, everyone has more fun out there. No one wants to lose every game they play. It's very discouraging, and just not fun for them.

On my Gardnerville team I had one boy that became so good at this, and he had so much respect from the other boys, I could let him run the drills while I went over to talk to a parent or one of my coaches. He was like an extra coach on the team. Do you know what he is doing now? He coaches, and works with the local youth football teams in his area.

Respect

Explain to your son or daughter the roles of the referee's, and the head coach. Only the head coach should question the referee when he believes that a there has been a mistake, or a rules interpretation problem.

Sometimes the referee was just out of position to see what happened. When you teach your son or daughter respect for the rules, then you teach them respect for law and order later in their life. Remember the example YOU set by your actions may influence the way THEIR life turns out. Many times, at the youth Soccer level as a coach if you are reasonable with a referee, and ask him to consult with one of the other referee's, he may reverse his opinion. They may have had a better view of the play. What usually happens though when the players, coaches, and parents start screaming, and complaining about the call, he will favor the other team on anything that is questionable or close. It's just human nature. In the long run it is better to just let the referee make his call. After the game is over, or the next day, then go to your head coach and tell him why you think the refereeing was poor. Your head coach should then go to the head of referee's, and explain the complaint. It might just be that the referee is inexperienced, new, or just doesn't understand the rules. But he will never improve if the head of referee's does not know that he has problems, and helps him correct them. Believe me, he never will change by your hollering, and screaming, at him. And it will just aggravate you and everyone else.

Hustle

Hustle will improve their attitude, and make the game better to watch. A little game you can play, with your son or daughter, is whenever you are working with them say, "Lets see how fast you can do this, maybe you can beat me". Then do it yourself as fast as you can, and afterwards ask them to try. Then no matter how fast they do it say, "Gee your almost as fast as me". When you see that they are getting faster, offer them some kind of reward like taking them to a movie on the weekend. Your son or daughter needs to be taught how to run fast. When substitutions are made they will need to run, on and off the field, fast to avoid delaying the game. When there is a lot of hustle the game goes faster, and mom that will sometimes get you home a lot earlier to start supper. I have personally proven to myself that hustling in life, at whatever your job is, impresses the boss also. So it's a good lesson to learn.

Health Habits

It is a very good idea to start them out in life with good health habits. What we are talking about here is plenty of sleep, a good nutritious balanced diet, with timely exercise, and conditioning. What we mean by timely is, don't over exercise them a few hours before game time. Not being tired, or sick, will improve their mental outlook, and attitude during the game.

Just a few words here about dietary supplements. **DO NOT** let them take anything containing *"Ephedra"*. In some cases it may be ok, but it has very serious side effects. Death being one. So why take a chance. They are young, so let them develop naturally for the long term.

I have had kids come to a summer afternoon, or early evening, game really dragging their feet, so to speak. And after talking to them I found out mom let them go over to a friends house all morning at their swimming pool. Swimming is a good workout, but not the day of a game. They need at least one days rest, from any heavy exercise before a game. As training for a sport these days becomes more complex the trainers, and strength coaches, have found that some exercises can be dangerous. So what I have tried to do is find out the latest techniques, and tailor the exercises to fit young kids practicing, and playing soccer.

cer it takes lots of stamina, and endurance, to play at the ntil the end of the game. In the later stages of the game, antage going for them. To be able to do this, young kids onditioning constantly. Do not over do it, but keep at it w repetitions. If your son or daughter is on the overweight t to over work them, or push them to hard. Especially rcise. You only increase repetitions when you see that e, and can handle it. If there is any question, talk to your

of techniques, to help the kids keep their strength level st teams go through a warm up exercise routine, just get them loosened up. So don't worry about exercising for the game. We had some kids that appeared to lose e, eat a banana the day before a game. This is to let the ystems by game time. Now days they have *"GatorAid"* here would be to give your son or daughter some a bottle with you, when you are out working with them We had one coach that had one of the parents cut up out to suck on during break. Both the bananas, and it then when they came out with *"GatorAid",* that worked hey are thirsty during practice, or during a game. Also plenty of water when it's hot out.

The Fundamentals

the basic skills needed, to be able to play the game of anning, dribbling, juggling, passing, trapping/receiving, ng, shooting, tackling, blocking, faking, and goal keeping. Even though it would be good to teach your son or daughter all of these skills, I am going to break them down for you into how they relate to the different positions. The reason being that most kids will not be able to master all of these basic skills, or positions. If you can't, in your mind, figure out what position they might be good at, then teach them strength, speed, and coordination. They can always use these skills no matter where they play. As an example if your son or daughter is very big for their age, with a large boned frame, and comes from a large boned family, they will probably end up being a goal keeper, or a defender, at the youth level. And mom or dad you will probably have to make the decision on what size it appears they will become when they get older

Try and imagine what position he or she might fit in when they get to high school age, then match them up with the possible position examples we will give you. Look at your parents, and see what kind of body structure they have. Moms, most of the time your son will inherit a similar structure to you, and your father. Your daughter, on the other hand, will probably be the size of your husband. You dads, whatever you do, don't try to make your son or daughter into a player at a position you always wanted to be in. Most of the time your son will take after his mothers side of the family, and your daughter will take after your side of the family. Dads you may be big and tall, but more than likely if your wife is smaller in size, your son will be smaller than you are. Your daughter, on the other hand, will probably be big and tall like you. Although these days there is always many exceptions. Take all of this into account when you decide what to start training them as. After a few years if it appears they are changing into a different size, skill level, or body structure than you imagined, you can always teach them the additional skills they will need. So, as an example, don't spend a lot of time teaching them how to kick goals if they are going to end up goal keeper. Spend it more wisely on improving their strength, speed, and coordination, at this young age.

When they get to their first team, it is very important that they know the fundamentals, for the position the coach is most likely to play them in. Such as Offense, Defense, goal keeper, defender, midfielder, forward, back, winger, or striker. This way the coach can spend more time on teaching the plays, formations, and tactics, they will be using in the game.

Forwards, Strikers and Wingbacks

The fundamental skills that forwards, strikers, and wingbacks, need are quickness, agility, speed, dribbling, passing, trapping/receiving, leg strength, kicking, shooting, heading, and faking. In the section on "Drills and Exercises", you will find out how to teach your son or daughter these skills. Probably the ones you need to concentrate on are dribbling first, then shooting, then after that quickness, then speed. Last teach them trapping/receiving, followed by passing, then heading, then leg strength, then faking.

Forwards, strikers, and wingbacks, **_can not_** use their hands or arms. They must start out at an early age, and work very hard to learn how to use their feet for dribbling, passing, trapping/receiving, and kicking. Where teaching them agility comes in, they need to learn how to move away from their opponent sometimes from side to side, or over the top of them, to be able to break free towards the goal. It also comes in handy in moving backwards when a pass to them has been intercepted, and they have to change quickly to defense. Quickness, and speed, will help them with their passing, and faking as well as avoiding their opponent. Working on their leg strength will help them from being knocked down by a tackle, and with kicking the ball harder, and farther . A special skill to look for here is a boy, or girl that is very coordinated, fast, and appears to already have an aggressive quality in their character.

Midfielders, Left Midfielders, and Right Midfielders

The fundamental skills all midfielders need are quickness, agility, speed, dribbling, passing, leg strength, trapping/receiving, and kicking. Also with those skills, they need to learn how to be very creative. Along with all the other skills, they need to have lots of endurance, and be the hardest working players on the team. In the section on "Drills and Exercises", you will find out how to teach your son or daughter these skills. They need to be able to create scoring opportunities. Look for open players to pass to. Quickly moving the ball around an opponent, and up the field. Concentrate on strength first, then endurance, then quickness. Follow that with dribbling, passing, trapping/receiving, kicking, leg strength, and last creativity. However, in any order you teach them, make sure they work on all of these skills. Since they are probably on the field longer, and they travel the longest distances of any of the players, really work hard on their endurance. And while doing that make sure they get plenty of "Gator Aid", to replenish the lost vitamin's, and minerals sweated out. Working on leg strength will help them to kick a pass farther up the field. Another thing to look for in a potential midfielder is, notice if they are naturally an aggressive, smart, and a rough and tumble type of boy, or girl. This is because the middle of the field is where the roughest, and toughest, part of the game occurs.

Defenders, Center Defenders (Stoppers), Center Backs, and Fullbacks

The fundamental skills defenders, center backs, and fullbacks (left and right backs) need are, quickness, agility, tackling, blocking, passing, speed, leg strength, and kicking. Concentrate on quickness first, then agility. Follow that with tackling, then blocking, then after that passing, then speed. Next leg strength, and kicking. Also a center back needs to be really rough, and tough. This is because the center part of the field gets very rough while they attempt to tackle, and block their opponent. Also they do need to be good at trapping/receiving, to intercept any long kicks in their area of the field. As a defender they need to become very good at marking (Covering an opponent). This is a special skill to learn because it is difficult for young kids to learn how to mark opponents, without fouling them. They will also need to learn the difference between "Man to Man" marking, and "Zone" marking. The section on "Drills and Exercises", will show you how to teach them the skills they need. If you have a son that is big, agile, tough, and appears to have good coordination, he might make a good defender. If they are small to medium in size, they still might make a good center back, or fullback as long as they have all the other skills. The fullback needs to be fast because on attack they have to move quickly down the sides (flanks) of the field. Leg strength here is important because when attempting to make a tackle, your leg has to be strong, to get the ball away from the opponent. Good leg strength may help in preventing a leg injury when they have been kicked hard. If they have a defensive trait and like to protect their friends, or worry about them, it will help them to become a good defender.

Sweeper

A sweeper, just like a goalkeeper, is a very specialized position. The fundamental skills they need are quickness, speed, agility, trapping/receiving, passing, tackling, leg strength, and kicking. Concentrate on quickness first, then speed. Follow that with agility, then tackling, then passing. Next trapping/ receiving, followed by leg strength, then last kicking. In order to get any ball missed by a defender, in front of them, they also need to be very self disciplined, and focused. The section on "Drills and Exercises", will show you how to teach them the skills they need. If your son or daughter is big for his age, or even medium size, coordinated, very agile, quick, and smart, they might make a good sweeper. If they have a defensive trait, and like to protect their friends, it will help them become a good defender. Good leg strength will help in kicking, and preventing a leg injury when they have been kicked hard. Toughness is another good trait to look for in them because they will be attacked very hard by opponents down near the penalty area, and the goal line. If they have all the skills, except they are very small, it may work for the beginning levels of play. Not later on though because they will be over powered.

Goalkeeper

The fundamental skills a goalkeeper needs are, quickness, agility, catching, passing, throwing, leg strength, and kicking. Concentrate on quickness first, then agility. Next catching, then throwing, then passing. Follow that with leg strength, and last kicking. In addition to all of these skills, your son or daughter will need to be mentally tough, and develop very quick reactions. The section on "Drills and Exercises", will show you how to teach them the skills they need. They will need lots of quickness, to get to fast incoming balls. They will need the agility, to change directions if they have been faked out of position. If your son or daughter is naturally a big roughhouse type of kid, tough, and is coordinated for their age, these skills will help make them a good goalkeeper. If they are quick, smart in school, and have a lot of energy compared to their friends, those natural skills will also help them to become a good goalkeeper. Not being afraid to dive way out to their left or right, is a skill that you may have to work very hard with them to develop. Staying alert, paying attention to the game, not getting bored standing around, may all be traits that will have to be developed. They must also learn to be "thick skinned", so to speak, and not worry or fret about it if they make a mistake.

Organize your Teaching

To organize your teaching, have a plan. My suggestion is sit down, read the section in the book where I talk about what fundamentals your son or daughter needs to learn. Then go through the rest of the book, and read the sections where I show the exercises, drills, and skills, needed. As you go through the book, start a _list_ of what they need to practice. Next to that particular drill or exercise, figure out approximately how much time will be needed to accomplish the teaching and practicing, then write it down. This way you can plan your teaching sessions. I am sure that when you get done, you will see that it takes a lot of hours to go through the fundamentals they need to learn, even for one time through. And with the few hours each week their coach has to go over fundamentals, time runs out, and they have to start working more on strategies, tactics, and formations. So teaching them at home from 5 years old, even a little each year, will really help them improve on their skills, and make it more fun.

Drills and Exercises

How do they help

Modern soccer training, and conditioning, is advancing all the time. In this book we will follow the latest recommended exercises, and tailor them for the younger kids. Over the past several years, researchers and physicians have identified exercises that are commonly used that can, in some cases, be potentially harmful to the body. These exercises can be modified, to eliminate the undesirable characteristics. This book will now use the safer alternatives.

I will break them down into the fundamental categories, and how they relate to what you want to teach. We will use picture figures, and diagrams as much as possible, to eliminate some of the confusion for all mothers, and some fathers, who may never have played the game of soccer. So, bear with us, those of you that have played a lot of soccer. This book was written as a reference book for mom and dad to use in teaching, and training, their son or daughter the skills of playing soccer. You can take the book right out in the yard with you, to look at for reference. I might suggest that if your son or daughter does not seem to be very interested in exercising, then try to make a game out of it. For instance say something to them like, "I bet you can't do this better than me", or "I bet you can't beat me down to the fence". Then do the exercise slow, and let them run a little bit ahead of you. Well you know what I mean. This will keep them interested. Whatever you do, get them into exercising at home. They will need to be well conditioned to play soccer. And, not only that, it will condition them to do exercises even as they grow older in life.

Warm up and Stretching

You need to warm up before doing any flexibility stretching, or exercising. Before starting, slowly jog around the area, or yard, for about 1 to 3 minutes to get the muscles warmed up. This is required before you start any of these flexibility stretching exercises. The shorter time is for the little 5-7 year olds. The longer time is for 12 year olds. Adjust the time accordingly with all the ages in between. Start with the upper part of the body stretches, and end up with the lower body part stretches last. Also after vigorously stretching, and exercising unless you are going to the strengthening exercises next, be sure to do a "COOL DOWN" routine, instead of just stopping cold.

Exercise No. 1- Overhead Stretch

FIGURE 1

This stretching exercise is for the torso, upper back, and rib cage. From the standing position, have them put their feet apart about shoulder width. Put the right hand on the right hip. Put the left arm straight up towards the sky and make a fist. Then keeping the arm as straight as possible, move it over until it touches the left ear. Next twist the wrist so it is pointing to the right. Then bend the whole upper body to the right, and hold the first time, for about 4 seconds. Totally relax for 3 or 4 seconds, in between each stretch. For all following stretches, hold for 7 seconds each. Next switch arms and do it to the left. Repeat at least 3 times with each arm *(SEE FIGURE 1)*.

Exercise No. 2- Seated Pelvic Stretch

This stretching exercise is for the lower back, obliques, and gluteus maximus. From the sitting position, have them put the left leg straight out in front with the toe up. Then put the right leg over the left, just back of the knee, with toes pointed outward. Next put the left arm on the right knee, with the left hand on the right hip. Then put the right arm out to the side, and slightly back. Turn the head to the right, and hold for 4 seconds the first time. Totally relax for 3 or 4 seconds, in between each stretch. For all following stretches, hold for 7 seconds each. Repeat this at least 3 times to each side *(SEE FIGURE 2)*.

FIGURE 2

Exercise No. 3- Hip Stretch

This stretching exercise is for the hip extensor muscles. From the lying position head down, have them put the left leg straight out to the front, toe down. Then lift the right leg up, keeping as straight as possible with the foot flat. Next

17

grasp the right leg with both hands, and pull back towards the head. Hold that position for about 4 seconds the first time. Totally relax for 3 or 4 seconds, in between each stretch. For all following stretches, hold for 7 seconds each. Repeat this at least 3 times with each leg *(SEE FIGURE 3)*.

Exercise No. 4- Active Hip Stretch

This stretching exercise is for the hip muscles. From the standing position, have them kick up the right leg and touch their right fingers. They should be up on their toes on the left leg.

FIGURE 3

Then have them totally relax for 3 or 4 seconds. Next switch, and kick up with the left leg. Do this at least 3 times with each leg *(SEE FIGURE 4)*.

Exercise No. 5- Seated Straddle Groin Stretch

This stretching exercise is for the inner thigh groin muscles. From the sitting position, have them put both legs way out to the side, toes up, keeping the knees down and straight.

FIGURE 4

Next have them grasp both hands together at the thumbs, then keeping the arms straight, lean forward, and reach way out in front. While doing this, try to keep the back straight. Hold that position for about 4 seconds the first time. Totally relax for 3 or 4 seconds, in between each stretch. For all following stretches, hold for 7 seconds each. Repeat this at least 3 times *(SEE FIGURE 5)*.

FIGURE 5

Exercise No. 6- Abductors Stretch

This stretching exercise is for abductors in the legs. From the standing position, have them put their right arm down at their side, and extend the left leg out to the top edge of a chair, or some other stationary item. Whatever the item is, the leg has to be as straight out to the side as possible. Then push lightly down, with the left hand just above the left knee. Hold that position for about 4 seconds the first time. Totally relax for 3 or 4 seconds, in between each stretch. For all following stretches, hold for 7 seconds each. Repeat this at least 3 times for each leg *(SEE FIGURE 6)*.

FIGURE 6

Exercise No. 7- Hip Extensor Stretch

FIGURE 7

This stretching exercise is for the front thigh muscles. From the kneeling position, have them put their left leg out in front, and extend the right leg to the rear. Then make sure the right knee is touching down while extending as far back as possible. Both hands should be out at the sides, palms down. This position is similar to a runners start. Then they lean forward until they feel the pull in the front thigh. If they don't feel much of a pull, then have them move the knee back farther until they do. Then Hold that position for about 4 seconds the first time. Totally relax for 3 or 4 seconds, in between each stretch. For all following stretches, hold for 7 seconds each. Repeat at least 3 times for each leg *(SEE FIGURE 7)*.

Exercise No. 8- Knee to Chest Stretch

This stretching exercise is for the knee, and lower back muscles. From the lying position, have them put the right leg straight out front, with toes up. Then have them pull their left leg up tight to their chest, with both hands grasped together just below the knee. Hold that position for about 4 seconds the first time. Totally relax for 3 or 4 seconds, in between each stretch. For all following stretches, hold for 7 seconds. Repeat this at least 3 times for each leg *(SEE FIGURE 8)*.

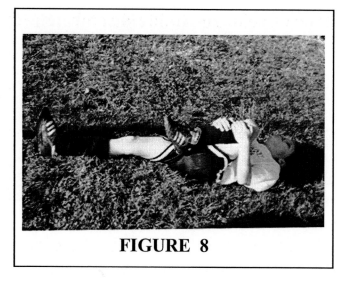

FIGURE 8

Exercise No. 9- Calf Stretch

This stretching exercise is for the calf muscles. From the kneeling position, have them lean forward and put both hands at their sides, palms down. Next have them extend the right leg straight out to the rear, and up off the ground. Then have them lift up the left knee and move it slightly forward of the hip, with toes bent down. This is like a modified runners start position. They should push to the rear until they feel pull in the calf muscle. Hold that position for about 4 seconds the first time. Totally relax for 3 or 4 seconds, in between each stretch. For all following stretches, hold for 7 seconds. Repeat this at least 3 times for each leg *(SEE FIGURE 9)*.

FIGURE 9

Exercise No. 10- Ankle Stretch

This stretching exercise is for ankle area muscles, and tendons. From the sitting position, have them put both feet, relaxed toes up, out in front of them with feet together. Arms out at their sides, for balance. Next keeping the legs flat to the floor or ground, have them roll both ankles forward, pushing the toes down. Hold that position for several seconds, then relax the feet back to the starting

FIGURE 10

position. Next, keeping the heels flat to the floor, have them roll both ankles back towards their head, with the toes pointing up. This should be a hard pull, with the toes hard towards their head. Hold that position for about 4 seconds the first time. Totally relax for 3 or 4 seconds in between each stretch. For all following stretches, hold for 7 seconds. Repeat this at least 3 times for each leg *(SEE FIGURE 10)*

Drills for Coordination and Agility

These drills are designed to teach them how to move around on their feet better, and change directions quickly, without falling down. These drills will help their balance, and agility, to improve. Soccer can be a rough game, especially in the middle of the field where kids can get tangled up with each other. They have to learn how to tumble, jump over, and roll over if they fall. If they do fall, they have to be able to come up on their feet, and keep moving. Coordination also includes good timing. As an example when a ball is kicked in the air, they have to have a very good sense of timing in order to get right where it comes down, to execute a header. Also dribbling and carrying the ball, with out looking at it, are coordination skills. If they will do these drills every day, even just for a short while, you will notice their coordination and field sense improving after just a few weeks.

Drill No. 1 Crossover Foot

This is called the crossover foot, and side to side exercise. Take your son or daughter out in the backyard, or down to the park where there is grass and lots of room. Stand in front of them, and face each other, at about three yards apart. You do the same steps they do, except start out to your right (a mirror image). Start by both of you walking through this slowly until you learn how to move your feet, then speed up little by little until you both get better at it. Start with the feet apart, then have them step to the left, with the left foot. Next step to the left, with their right foot crossing over the top of their left foot. Then step again to the left, with their left foot crossing behind their right foot. Next step again to the left, with their right foot crossing behind their left foot. Then step again to the left, with their left foot over the top of their right foot. Then keep repeating this combination of steps to the left, over and over, for about 30 yards. Then stop and

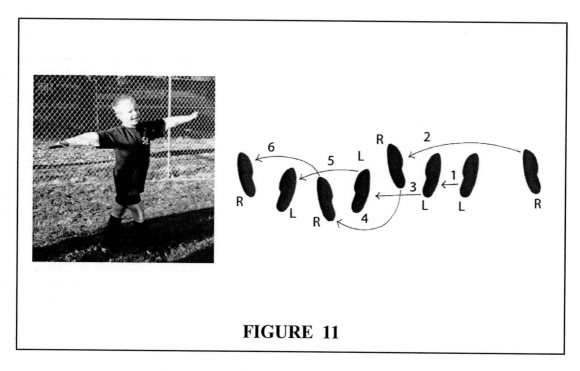

FIGURE 11

reverse these steps, going first to their right, with their right foot, then with their left foot over their right, and so on, for about 30 yards to the right. Keeping their hands straight out to their sides will help them keep their balance. The better they get at doing this, you can speed the process up little by little. After a few weeks, your son or daughter should be able to do this drill on the run, and without falling down. If not, keep working with them, and don't give up because they can learn it *(SEE FIGURE 11)*.

Drill No. 2 Running Backwards

This is called the running backwards coordination exercise. Here you will need to find a very large back yard, or a big area in a park, with thick grass. The

FIGURE 12

reason I am suggesting thick grass is, it will cushion their fall a little if they fall backwards. This exercise will help them back peddle, and change directions while marking an opponent.

First both you, and your son or daughter, line up side by side about 3 or 4 yards apart, with about 50 yards of clear space behind you. Then both of you start running backwards while pumping your arms up and down. Do this for about 50 yards, then stop and repeat the drill for about 50 yards, back to where you started. Usually one, or both, of you will fall down the first few times you try this drill. If either of you fall down, laugh and make a joke out of it. If you criticize them too much, they may not want to do it any more. If they are falling down a lot, and you are not, then you may want to fall down a few times yourself so that they will see it is hard for you also, and not be discouraged. This usually works in keeping them interested. Also shout encouragement to them as you are running side by side. The secret for keeping their balance is, raising their knees high while pumping their hands up and down as fast as they can. Once he, or she, can run fast for the 50 yards, and not fall down, you will notice their interest level go up. When they do become good at this, then you can change the drill a little to make it harder. Some suggestions, on how to do this, might be to have them run backwards about 10 or 15 yards, then blow a whistle and have them turn around without stopping, and run forward. Keep doing this, and change directions every 10 or 15 yards. This is one of the best drills for kids, that I have seen, that will really improve their running coordination and agility *(SEE FIGURE 12).*

Drill No. 3 Monkey Walk

This is called the monkey walk drill. Take your son or daughter out to where there is a large area of grass, and have them get down on all fours, not on their knees though. The fingers of both hands should be spread out, and they should be up on the balls of their feet. Then have them walk on all fours to the front, then backwards, and from side to side. As they get a little more

FIGURE 13

comfortable with this position, then stand in front of them, and point with your hand to all the different directions you want them to go in. Then have them speed it up, little by little until they become very good at reacting to your direction changes. After a few weeks, they should begin to get better at this, and will think it is fun as long as you don't criticize them, or push them to hard. This drill is very good at helping them move around on the ground, and getting up very fast when knocked on the ground *(SEE FIGURE 13)*.

Drills for Controlled Falling & Field Presence

These drills are designed to help kids control their body, and react to falling, so they won't get hurt. No matter what position they play, they must learn how to roll, jump, and control, their body while falling. The more they do these drills, the more natural it will be for them to tumble, roll, or jump over if they start to fall. Repetition of these drills will make these reactions a habit.

Drill No. 4- Forward Roll

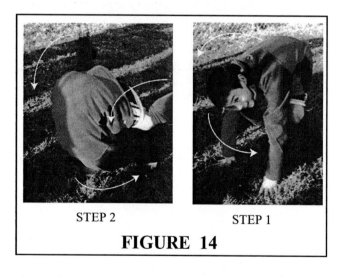

STEP 2   STEP 1

FIGURE 14

This is just a simple roll, or forward somersault. Have your son or daughter stand with their feet slightly spread, and bend at their knees a little, then from the waist bend over, and put their hands on the ground. Next have them put their head between their legs, and just fall forward rolling over. Have them do this a lot in slow motion before doing it fast. After they get better at this, have them do the drill from a short running start. If they are not good at this, then have them do the drill, over and over, step by step until they do get better at it. An inexperienced boy or girl could jam their neck, or hurt their shoulder if they try to do this roll from the start, at a full run. So make sure, he or she, can do it naturally standing still before you ever let them do it at a full run. It is probably better to start out your approach, at just a few steps head start, and increase the *run up distance* little by little *(SEE FIGURE 14)*.

Drill No. 5- Backward Roll

STEP 1   STEP 2

FIGURE 15

This is a simple backwards roll, or somersault. Have your son or daughter stand with their feet apart, and bend at their knees a little, with both arms at their side, and bent upwards just a little bit. Next have them sit down, and just as they do, then bring their knees to their chest, and thrust both arms backwards over their shoulders. Then all they have to do is roll over backwards, using their hands on the ground, to push the rest of their body through the roll, then coming up on their feet. Have them try this a lot, in slow motion before doing it fast. For some reason this always seems to be harder than the forward roll, for young kids to do. If this is the case with your son or daughter, then someone needs to stand, or kneel to the side of them, and use their hands to help flip them over and through the roll. After you are sure they have mastered the technique, have them run slowly backwards a little bit, then fall and do the roll. They can speed it up, little by little as they get better at it. This is so they can learn what the reaction to falling backwards while on the move is, then rolling out of the fall, and coming up on their feet *(SEE FIGURE 15)*.

Drill No. 6 Shoulder Roll

This is called the shoulder roll. It is just like the forward roll in drill No. 4, except you roll over the right, or the left shoulder. Have your son or daughter stand feet apart, bend at their knees a little, then bend over from the waist, and put their right hand down on the ground. Next they just fall forward, and as they do, put their head between their legs, and the right knee down on the ground. Next they just roll over their right shoulder, and try to come up on their feet. Have them try this a lot, in slow

STEP 2   STEP 1

FIGURE 16

motion before trying to do it fast. The difference between this drill, and the regular forward roll is, he or she will be rolling over one or the other shoulder, instead of their back. The left shoulder roll is the same, except they will roll over their left shoulder, with their left knee and arm down. The left shoulder roll may be harder for them to learn if they are right handed, and right shoulder harder if they are left handed. So be patient with him or her if one side seems to be harder than the other for them to learn. If they are having trouble try standing, or kneeling, next to them, and help flip them over with your hands until they gets the feel of it. When you are sure they have mastered the roll over both shoulders, then have them run a few steps forward, fall forward, and do a roll. First over their right shoulder, then their left. You can speed this up, little by little as they get better at it. All of this is so they experience the reaction to falling, and rolling, to the right or left while moving around *(SEE FIGURE 16)*.

Drill No. 7- Over the Top Jumping Drill

This is a jumping over someone drill. This is a drill to teach them to go over the top, of players falling in front of them. You will need a friend, about the same size as your son or daughter, to practice this drill. You will also need a thick soft grass area, in the yard or park, to work in. This is so they won't get hurt if they accidentally fall. Wearing their shin

FIGURE 17

guards, will protect their lower legs on this drill. Have the friend stand, and bend over at the waist. Then have your son or daughter go behind them about 5 yards. Next they start running, at a medium speed, towards the back of the friend, and leap frog over the top of them. They will do this by jumping up, and place both of their hands on the back of the friend. Then push down with the hands, and swing the legs through as they go over. This may take some work with the real little kids. Maybe just have them run slowly, put their hands down, and jump over an imaginary person until they get the feel of it. Then you can have the friend get down lower, on all fours, to make it easier for them to get over. Also you can speed up the running as they get better at this. Keep working with them until they master this drill *(SEE FIGURE 17)*.

Drill No. 8- Over the Rolling Body Drill

This is a drill for jumping up, and clearing a rolling body. What this does is, teach them to go over the top of players, rolling sideways, in front of them. You will need a friend, about the same size as your son or daughter, to practice this drill. You will also need to find a thick soft grass area, in the yard or park, to work in. The grass is so they won't get hurt if they accidentally fall. Wearing their shin guards, will protect their lower legs on this drill.

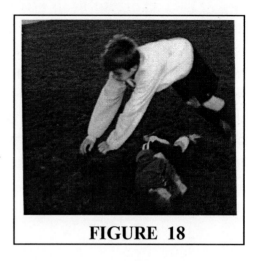

FIGURE 18

Have the friend lay down on the ground, flat on their stomach. Have your son or daughter stand about 3 yards to the left of the friend, and back about 3 yards. On the word "GO", have the friend roll, over and over, on the ground to their left, and past a line straight in front of where your son or daughter is standing. Also on the word "GO", have your son or daughter start to run slowly straight ahead. When they see the rolling friend, start to pass just to their right, they jump up and kick both feet backwards, letting the friend roll underneath them and on by. They should come down on all fours, push up with the hands, and start running forward again. After the friend stops rolling, have your son or daughter go back to the original starting position. Then again on the word "GO" , the friend starts rolling back to their right. At the same time your son or daughter runs forward, lets the rolling friend pass underneath, from their left side, then jumps up just as before and comes down on all fours. Then they Push up again, and run forward. As they get better at this drill, have them always look straight ahead, and not at the rolling friend. This helps them develop their peripheral vision *(SEE FIGURE 18)*.

Drills for Strength

These drills are designed to build up, and strengthen, your son or daughters key body muscles, mainly in the legs. Many young kids these days just sit around home a lot, and *don't* have a lot of chores to do as they did years ago, possibly on a farm. And because they have very little to do, with their arms or legs, like pitch hay, or carry buckets of milk, and things like that they are weak. It is important that they do some of these drills every day. If they get tired and quit for a week or two, the drills will not help them as much. Follow all breathing instructions, for they are also important in each drill.

Drill No. 9- Sit up Crunches

This exercise is to strengthen the abdominal, or stomach muscles. Have your son or daughter lay down on the floor, on their back, with both knees bent up about 10 to 12 inches high, and feet on the floor. They should then fold both arms , in an "X", across their chest. Next have them raise up just enough to get their neck, and shoulder top, off the floor a little bit. Then hold the raised up position for 5 seconds. Each time, just before they sit up, have them take a deep breath and then exhale it very slowly while they sit up and hold. These can be done with someone holding down their feet for balance, **but only** if they can't raise up, without the help. Start out by having them do about 5 or 10 if they can do that many. If they are a large boy or girl, still carrying a lot of baby fat, they may not be able to do that many. In that case start them out with the most they can easily do, without struggling too much, and increase the numbers as they get stronger **(SEE FIGURE 19)**.

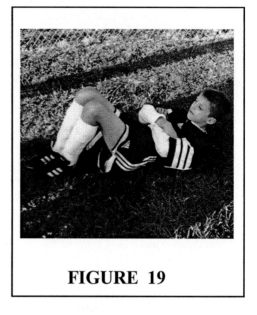

FIGURE 19

Drill No. 10- Leg lifts

This is another exercise to strengthen the abdominal, or stomach muscles. Either you, mom or dad, or another person will have to help out here. Have your son or daughter lay down on the floor, on their back, with both legs straight out in front, with feet together. Have the helper stand just behind their head. Next have them reach back, and grasp both ankles of the helper. Then lift both feet up, with the knees bent, until the buttocks are raised up off the floor. Each time, just before they raise the legs up, have them take a deep breath and hold it for at least 5 seconds while they raise the legs all the way up Then have them expel the air as they come back down, into the lying position. Start out by having them do about 5 or 10, if they can do that many. If they are a large boy or girl, still carrying a lot of baby fat, they may not be able to do that many. In that case, start them out with the most they can easily do, without struggling too much, and increase the numbers as they get stronger *(SEE FIGURE 20)*.

Drill No. 11- Half Squats

FIGURE 20

This exercise is to strengthen the quadriceps (front thigh), hamstrings, gluteal (buttocks), and back muscles. Have your son or daughter stand, with both hands on their hips, and feet slightly apart. Next have them squat halfway down, keeping their balance. They should take a deep breath before they squat, and hold that position for at least 5 seconds. Also let me point out that they should bend back far enough to feel the tightening in their front, and back thigh muscles. Then as they straighten back up to the starting position, they slowly expel the air. Have them start out by doing about 3 or 5 of these. If they are a large boy or girl, still carrying a lot of baby fat, they may not be able to do that many. In that case, start them out with the most they can easily do, without struggling too much, and increase the numbers as they get stronger *(SEE FIGURE 21)*.

FIGURE 21

Drill No. 12- Wall Sits

This is another exercise to strengthen the quadriceps (front thigh), hamstrings, gluteal (buttocks), and back muscles. Have your son or daughter stand, next to a wall, then put both feet together about 1-1/2 feet out in front of them. Next they put both hands on their knees, and slide their back down the wall until their thighs are about parallel to the floor. They should take a deep breath before they slide down the wall, then hold the down position for at least 5 seconds. Also let me point out, they should slide down far enough to feel a tightening in their front, and back thigh muscles. Then as they straighten back up to the starting position, they slowly expel the air, then relax for half a minute or

FIGURE 22

so. Have them start out by doing about 3 or 5 of these. If they are a large boy or girl, still carrying a lot of baby fat, they may not be able to do that many. In that case, start them out with the most they can easily do, without struggling too much, and increase the numbers as they get stronger *(SEE FIGURE 22)*.

Drill No. 13- Knee Bend Pulls

This exercise is to strengthen the knees. The exercise is going to be a little harder to accomplish because you, mom or dad, will need a resistance type stretch band, and maybe another person to help out. Ideally, you also need an exercise bench in order that they can hold onto the front bar(s), and not slip backwards. The bench also gives you place for the non exercising foot to pull against. The right kind of stretch band is not easy to find. The cheapest, and maybe the best place, is on the "InterNet". Knees are probably at, or near, the top of the list for injuries. This means that if you can get set up to do this exercise with them, it will be a big help, and maybe keep them injury free.

To do the exercise, have your son or daughter lay down on their stomach, on top of the bench. Then have them hold on to the bars, at the front of the bench, with both hands. Attach the stretch band to something permanent. Next have them slip the free end of the band around their left ankle. They should take a deep breath before they pull the leg up, then hold the up position for at least 5 seconds. Then as they lower the leg to the starting position, they slowly expel the air. If you can't afford a bench, but you can get a band, you can still get set up to do this exercise.

In that case, what you might do is, cut off two broom stick handles about 9 inches in length. Find a place out in the back yard with plenty of grass, and space around it. Drive the

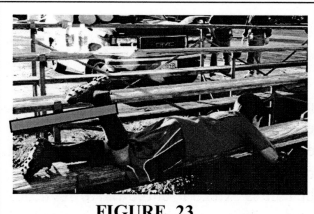
FIGURE 23

stakes about 4 inches into the ground, and about 12-14 inches apart. Have them lay down on their stomach, and hold on to the handles with each hand. Next have them extend both feet out behind them, with toes pointed down. Then have the helper get down on their knees, moving their left knee up against the sole of your son or daughters left foot, for support. Next the helper puts your son or daughters right ankle through one end of the stretch band, and holds the other end stationary. Then your son or daughter can go ahead and pull up with the right leg. Have them start out by doing about 3 or 5 of these with each leg *(SEE FIGURE 23)*.

Drill No. 14- Transverse Ab Strengthening

FIGURE 24

This exercise is to strengthen the transverse abdominal muscles. This exercise will take a lot of concentration, for little kids to do. So make sure they know, they have to be focused when they begin to start this exercise. Have your son or daughter get down on all fours, with arms and thighs perpendicular to the floor. Then have them take a deep breath, and as they exhale they pull their belly button up towards their back, and hold for 5 seconds. Nothing else moves except their belly. They should also keep a natural curve in their back while doing the exercise. Then they go back to the starting position, and relax for half a minute or so. Then repeat. Have them do at least 5 of these *(SEE FIGURE 24)*.

Drill No. 15- Dumbbell Pullover

This exercise is for the rectus abdominal muscles. Again, you will ideally need an exercise bench. However if you don't have a bench, you could do this exercise over the edge of a sturdy bed. You will also need a dumbbell, for this exercise. Have your son or daughter lay down on their back, on the bench (or bed), then stretch their legs out, with feet together. Move up, so their arms will be able to extend over the end of the bench (bed). Next take the dumbbell, and grasp with both hands together, just under the end bulb. Then take a deep breath, and lower the dumbbell behind them, over the end of the bench (bed) *SEE*

FIGURE 25-A. Then they pull up the dumbbell up, to a position just over their throat *(SEE FIGURE 25-B)*.

Cool Downs after Exercising

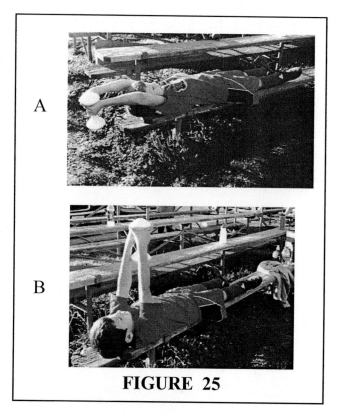

FIGURE 25

After their body gets all heated up, it tries to cool itself down after a workout. So make sure they do *"cool downs"* after doing any strenuous exercises, or drills. Cool downs can be as simple as slowly just walking around the yard, or pedaling very slowly and relaxed on an exercise bicycle, for at least 3-5 minutes. Or it could be just a slowed down, and relaxed, version of the strenuous exercise they just finished. The idea is, to get as many parts of the body moving, but in a slower motion for about 3-5 minutes, right after you have completed your exercise routine. Remember though, the more intense their exercise pace was, the more gradual their cool down pace should be. Step it down gradually. Another thing to point out is, don't let them get "chilled" right after a strenuous intense exercise routine, by being someplace where the temperature is cool. Such as outside when it's 50 or 60 degrees. Experts say the ideal temperature to cool down in is 68-72 degrees.

Drills for Dribbling

These drills are designed to improve their ability to move the ball around the playing field, with his or her feet. What we want to accomplish is, get them started on developing the techniques they will need to do their best. If they want to play any soccer position, except goalkeeper, they have to be able to dribble, and control the ball. After you teach them the basics, have them work on their dribbling skills constantly. Some kids will pick this up quickly, however most kids will have to really work at this, to become a good dribbler. If you start them out at 5 years old, they should be pretty good at it by High School age. Kids learn quickly, but they also forget quickly. The answer is, continuous repetition.

To learn dribbling, think of the ball as "glued to your foot". Where your foot goes, the ball has to be right there with it. Most young players will be inclined to dribble with their dominant foot. Right foot for right handed kids, left foot for left handed kids. Which is probably fine when they are 5 or 6 years old. Try to teach them to dribble with either foot. Because in the long run, they are a more rounded versatile player when they can dribble with either foot. It's sort of like the "switch hitter" in baseball. Where and how your foot meets the ball, will depend on which direction you want it to go. Don't dribble in a _croud_, or for too long a period time, look to pass the ball to get it up field quicker. Know where your team mates are, to make the pass. Basically the ball is dribbled, or controlled, 5 different ways with the feet.

FIGURE 26

1. The inside of the foot.
2. The outside of the foot.
3. The instep of the foot
4. The heel of the foot.
5. The sole of the foot.

Drill No. 16- Inside of the Foot

The Basics are:

Dribbling the ball, with the inside of the foot, is probably the most common and easiest way to move the ball around. Contact with the ball is made with the inside center, to the front, portion of the foot *(SEE FIGURE 26)*. Teach them to push, or dribble, in a line through the center part of the ball .After practicing for a week or two, try to get them to dribble the ball by feel while looking straight ahead. Move the ball, by pushing it no farther than one step away. Train them to look ahead 6 to 8 feet while dribbling. They also have to learn to develop their peripheral field of vision.

Practice:

To practice dribbling, you mom or dad will have to set up several courses for them to dribble in. These courses can be set up with cones *(SEE EQUIPMENT SECTION)*. Or if you can't afford to buy cones, you can make them using old, white plastic, 1 gallon mike bottles. Fill them with sand, kitty

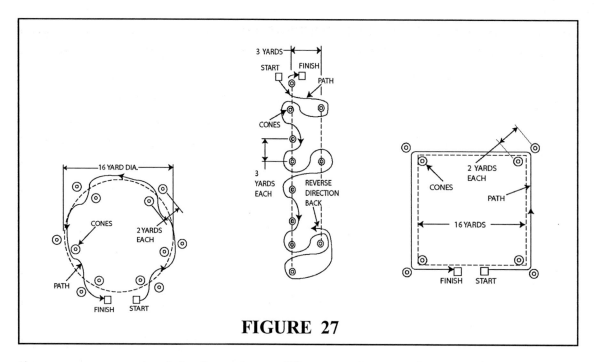

FIGURE 27

litter, or water, to weight them down. Then you just set them out in patterns, to make your course. There are three basic shapes of courses that you can set up. They are the circle, the square, and the slalom *(SEE FIGURE 27)*. Have them dribble, with the inside of the foot, through each course at least once each day. If they are having trouble navigating, it's probably because they are not hitting the ball in the right spot while trying to aim it with their foot. In that case, you will have to stop them, and go over in slow motion how they aim the ball. As an example if you hit the ball, just ahead of the center with the right foot, you push it more to the left. And if you hit it with the left foot, just ahead of center, it goes more to the right. So, if you want to keep the ball going straight, you probably want to use the right foot first, then the left foot next. This way, the ball will kind of zig zag it's way along straight ahead. If you keep hitting it with the same foot, over and over while moving forward, you will tend to go in a circle. Forwards, strikers, midfielders, fullbacks, wings, and wing backs, need to work hard on this as much as possible.

Drill No. 17- Outside of the Foot

The Basics are:

Dribbling the ball, with the outside of the foot, is probably the second most common way to move the ball around. Contact with the ball is made with the outside center, to the front, portion of the foot *(SEE FIGURE 28)*. Teach them to push, or dribble, in a line through the center part of the ball. After practicing for a week or two, try to get them to dribble the ball by feel while looking straight ahead. Move the ball, by pushing it no farther than one step away. Train them to look ahead 6 to 8 feet while dribbling. They also have to learn to develop their peripheral field of vision.

FIGURE 28

Practice:

To practice dribbling, you mom or dad will have to set up several courses for them to dribble in *(SEE FIGURE 27)*. These courses can be set up with cones, or plastic milk bottles *(SEE EQUIPMENT SECTION)*. Have them dribble with the outside of the foot, through each course at least once each day, if possible. Also as they dribble through the courses, have them alternate between the different types of dribbles. But only have them alternate after they have mastered each one of the different types of dribbles. If they are having trouble navigating, it's probably because they are not hitting the ball in the right spot while trying to aim it, with their foot. In that case, you will have to stop them, and go over in slow motion how they aim the ball. As an example if you hit the ball, just ahead of the center, with the right foot, you push it more to the right. And if you hit it with the left foot, just ahead of center, it goes more to the left. So, if you want to keep the ball going straight, you probably want to use the right foot first, then the left foot next. This way the ball will

FIGURE 29

kind of zig zag it's way along straight ahead. If you keep hitting it with the same foot, over and over while moving forward, you will tend to go in a circle. There is also another drill that will help them learn how to dribble, using the outside of the foot.

Have them face forward and side step, or slide, first to the right, then the left. They have to keep moving, and use their arms out to their sides, to keep their balance *(SEE FIGURE 29)*. All the time dribbling the ball in the same direction they are sliding. Forwards, midfielders, strikers, fullbacks, wings, and wing backs, need to work hard on the outside of the foot dribble as much as possible.

Drill No. 18- Instep of the Foot

The Basics are:

Dribbling the ball, with the instep, makes it easier to dribble straight ahead. Contact is made with the laces part of the shoe *(SEE FIGURE 30)*. This is probably the best way to move the ball, very quickly, down the field. How to accomplish this is as you make the kick swing of the foot, you just drop the toe down as you start to make contact. This should not

FIGURE 30

be to hard to learn because as you run, your feet are already pointing straight ahead anyway, and there is no need to twist the foot.

Practice:

To practice dribbling, with the instep of the foot, set up the square course *(SEE FIGURE 27)*. Or just have them dribble down the field, or an open space, for about 30 yards. And remind them, not to let the ball get more than one step ahead of them. Run along with them, and observe if they are contacting the ball right on the laces part of the shoe. This is a technique that forwards, midfielders, fullbacks, wings, and wig backs must learn. So have them work on this technique

FIGURE 31

every day if possible, especially if they are a forward. Forwards will probably use this style of dribble, more than any of the other players as they sprint in to kick a goal.

Drill no. 19- Heel of the Foot

The Basics are:

Dribbling the ball, with the heel, is almost like the hitting it with the inside of the foot. The difference is, you are hitting the ball with inside heel part of the foot *(SEE FIGURE 31)*. This is probably the least used contact place, on the foot. You may, on some occasions though, want to

FIGURE 32

move backwards with a short dribble. And you would use the back of the heel, with a light tap, to let an opponent coming in too fast, move on by *(SEE FIGURE 32)*. Again this is a technique not used to often. However midfielders should know how to do this.

Practice:

To practice this, have your son or daughter get out in an open field, then have them dribble straight ahead for about 5 yards, using the inside heel part of their foot. After 5 yards, have them stop the dribble quickly, with the sole of their foot, then tap the ball several times very lightly backwards, using the same foot they are dribbling with. Then have them stop the ball again, with the sole of their foot, and continue dribbling forward again. Make sure they practice this with both the right, and left feet. Have them work on this last, of the 5 different ways of dribbling.

Drill No. 20- Sole of the Foot

The Basics are:

Dribbling the ball, with the sole of the foot, is when you want to stop the ball, change direction very quickly, or slow down the dribble to a very slow pace. This is a must technique, for midfielders to use. The contact point, with the

FIGURE 33

ball, is made with the bottom (sole) part of the shoe *(SEE FIGURE 33)*.

Practice:

To practice this, have your son or daughter get out in an open field, then have them dribble straight ahead, using any style for about 5 yards. Then have them stop the dribble, using the bottom of their shoe. Once they have stopped the ball, have them move the ball directly to the right, then the left, using the bottom of their shoe. Then immediately dribble forward again for 5 yards, stop, then go sideways again. Keep repeating this 4 or 5 times, for practice. All players should learn how to do this because no matter where you are on the field, you just never know when you might have to stop the ball with your feet, and change directions very quickly.

Drills for Passing

These drills are designed to improve the ability of your son or daughter, to get the ball down the field quickly. What we want to accomplish is, get them started on developing the techniques they will need to learn, to improve their passing. If they want to play any soccer position, they have to be able to pass the ball to their team mates. After you teach them the basics, have them work on their passing skills constantly. Some kids will pick this up quickly, however most kids will have to be constantly reminded, and really work at this, to become a good passer. If you start them out at 5 years old, they should be pretty good at it by High School age. Kids learn quickly, but they also forget quickly. The answer is, continuous repetition. A point to remember is, dribbling is a technique to make room, so you can pass the ball. And you need the room, to see your team mates, so you can pass to them. You mom or dad, need to teach them to look out over the whole field before they even get the ball. This is so they know where their team mates, and the opposing players, are all generally located.

As I notice, by watching lots of the smaller youth teams play, almost every kid on the field is bunched up around the ball. And this is going to make it hard to dribble, or pass while in a croud. There is maybe 20 little feet, all kicking blindly at the ball. If you try to make a long kick pass, it will more than likely bounce off a player, and not go in the direction you kicked it in. Your best bet is to "holler" at your team mates to spread out. Then protect the ball, as best you can, and try to pick up one of your closest team mates, for a short pass. Or maybe a lob kick pass, over the croud, into a clear area. Bear in mind all you coaches reading this, I am talking about advice to 6 -8 year olds, out there playing on teams already.

One drill (or game) I have seen that will help them develop the necessary skills to keep the ball away from close by opponents, is called "Dribble Tag". One

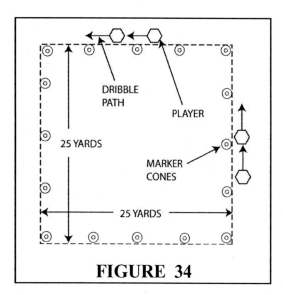

DRIBBLE PATH

PLAYER

25 YARDS

MARKER CONES

25 YARDS

FIGURE 34

of the passing skills needed is, learning to get away from opponents quickly, so you have room to pass the ball. To practice with them on this drill, you will need at least one, and preferably three, players the same size as your son or daughter, to help out on this. How this little game works is, take some cones *(SEE THE SECTION ON TYPICAL TRAINING EQUIPMENT)*, and mark a square field area about 25 yards long to a side *(SEE FIGURE 34)*. Ideally you should have four players, in groups of two, about two yards apart, spread out around the square and each one with a ball. At the word "GO", they all start out dribbling around the square. The object is, try to tag another player while moving around the square, and at the same time still controlling the ball. The rule is, you must control the ball, and you get 1 point every time you tag one of the other players. However, you lose 1 point every time another player tags you. Another rule is, you must move as quickly as possible as you dribble around the square. This game gets them in the habit of watching the field in front of them as well as where the other players are located. You can try this with 5-7 year olds, but I don't think they will be able to dribble good enough yet, in order to play this game.

There are many different types of passing techniques. In fact there are so many , that I am only going to cover the ones that are mainly used. In the United States, most youth coaches don't teach as many different types as they do in Europe. We will try to cover some, from each part of the world. The different types of passing kicks are:

1. The straight ahead instep type.
2. The inside part of the foot type.
3. The outside/ inside instep part of the foot (on the laces) type.
4. The outside part of the foot type.
5. The drop type.
6. The hip turn type.
7. The over the head (Bicycle) type.
8. The overlap run type.
9. The "give and go" type.

FIGURE 35

Other ways the ball can be passed, besides kicking, is heading, and pushing, using the feet, thighs, or knees. Lets start out with the kicking type first.

Drill No. 21- Straight Ahead Instep Pass

The Basics are:

Kicking the ball straight ahead, with the instep (laces), is probably the most powerful of the passing kicks. It should be used for long distance passes. Contact is made with the laces, and with the toe down *(SEE FIGURE 35)*. The foot swing is, into the center part of the ball, with the follow through going straight ahead, or directly at the target area or person. As they make contact with the ball, the body should be straight up and down, or slightly leaning back for very long passes.

Practice:

To practice this pass, find a large back yard, or field, to work on. Then have them start dribbling slowly straight ahead. Before they start, mom or dad, you go down the field, about 20 yards for the 5-8 year olds, and up to maybe 40 yards out for 12 year olds. Then have them kick an instep pass, straight ahead to you. Next mom or dad, move 10-20 to yards to each side of them, and have them kick a passes to you. Midfielders mostly, will need to learn this type of pass. All players though should learn how to make this pass if possible. Do this over and over until they can get the pass right to you. Have them kick pass to you standing still at first, then to you while you are on the move. If you are moving, the pass should lead you, so it comes just ahead of where you are running to. Watch them,

C   B   A

FIGURE 36

and make sure they are using the correct part of the foot. If not, stop and go over exactly how they should do it.

Drill No. 22- Inside Part of the Foot Pass

The Basics are:
Kicking the ball, with the inside part of the foot, is probably the most widely used pass in Soccer. It is mostly used for short, or medium range passes. Contact is made with the inside flat part of the foot *(SEE FIGURE 36-B)*. The ankle should be flexed, and rigid. With the foot still turned and rigid, the follow through should be through the center of the ball, and right towards the target area or player *(SEE FIGURE 36-C)*. The body should be upright, and squared towards the direction of the pass. Keep the non-kicking foot fairly close to the ball, for balance *(SEE FIGURE 36-A)*. How hard to kick the ball, will depend on the distance away the player receiving the pass is located. Too soft, and it won't get there. Too hard, and it may go way over their head, or past them.

Practice:
To practice this pass, find a large back yard, or field, to work on. Then have your son or daughter start dribbling slowly straight ahead. Before they start, mom or dad, you go down the field about 10-15 yards straight ahead of them, to receive the pass. Have them kick several passes to you with the right leg, then switch, and have them kick several passes with their left leg. Next mom or dad, go off first to the left, and to the right of them, about 5-10 yards. And have them start dribbling, then have them make short passes to you over to their left, and then right, taking turns with both legs to make the passes. Midfielders, center backs, fullbacks, and even defenders, must learn how to make this pass.

Drill No. 23- Outside/ Inside Instep Part of the Foot Pass

The Basics are:
Kicking the ball, with the inside or outside part of the instep, is very effective because it puts spin on the ball. This is something like a curve ball in Baseball. This type of pass can be a big help, in curving a pass around a defender. The body should be upright, and not tilted back while making contact. Contact is made with the inside instep part of the foot *(SEE FIGURE 37-B),* or the outside instep part of the foot *(SEE FIGURE 37-C)*. At the time of

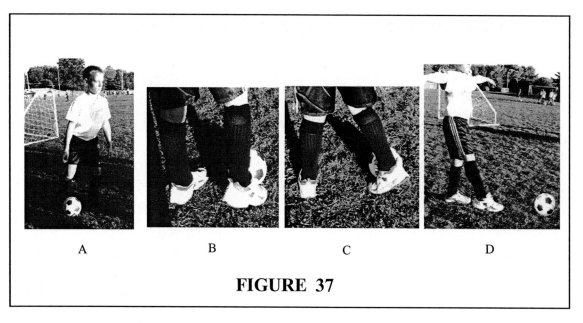

A   B   C   D

FIGURE 37

contact, the kicking leg should be slightly bent, with the ankle rotated either to the inside or the outside. The non-kicking leg should be slightly bent at the hip, ankle, and knee *(SEE FIGURE 37-A)*. In the follow through, the kicking leg should come to rest in front of the non-kicking leg, and at an angle *(SEE FIGURE 37-D)*. The whip snap action from the knee down, is really what puts the spin on the ball. A rotated hip snap though is what gives the ball distance. How hard to kick the ball, will depend on the distance away the player receiving the pass is located. Too soft, and it won't get there. Too hard, and it may go way over their head, or past them.

Practice:

To practice this pass, find a large back yard, or field, to work on. Then have your son or daughter start dribbling slowly straight ahead. Before they start, mom or dad, you go down the field about 20 yards for the 5-8 year olds, up to maybe 40 yards down field for 12 year olds. This is out straight ahead of them to receive their first passes. When they kick these passes to you, observe if the ball is curving. If not, then someone will have to stand next to them to find out what they are doing wrong. Make corrections and keep trying until they can do it right. Then, mom or dad, go out to the same distance as before, then to each side about 10-15 yards. At each side have them try to make an across the field curving kick pass to you, by aiming just a little to the side of you, so that it curves into you. Keep working with them until they can make it curve correctly. Midfielders, and really all backs, should work on and learn this technique.

Drill No. 24- Outside Part of the Foot Pass

The Basics are:

Kicking the ball, with the outside part of the foot, is mostly for little short "flick" type passes. This would be like when your team mate is just 5-10 yards to the side, or slightly ahead of you. And when you want to flip them a real quick little short pass. Contact is made with the outside part of the foot, usually between the center of the foot, and the toes *(SEE FIGURE 38)*. A little twisting ankle flick, along with a little quick snap of the leg, gets the ball over to a close by team mate, and very quickly. Where you strike the ball, with foot, depends on whether you want the ball to kind of loop over in the air, or roll more on the ground. Striking it at, or slightly above center, will make it roll. Striking it, below the center to the bottom, makes it go up. Your son or daughter will probably have to experiment a little, to get used to knowing just where to strike the ball, to make it do what they want it to do.

FIGURE 38

Practice:

To practice this pass, find a large back yard, or field, to work on. Then have your son or daughter start dribbling slowly straight ahead. Before they start, mom or dad, you go about 5 -10 yards to the left side of them, and maybe just slightly ahead of them. Then as you are both moving approximately side by side, have them flick a rolling pass over to you, using the outside of the left foot. Next switch sides to their right, then have them use the outside of their right foot to, flick a rolling pass to you over on the right side. After they master this technique a few times, have them do the same things, with each different foot. Except this time, they should make the ball loop over to you in the air, rather than on a roll on the ground. Keep working with them until they can make both of these passes correctly. Midfielders especially, but really all players, need to learn both of these techniques.

Drill No. 25- Drop Pass

The Basics are:

Kicking the ball, with the inside part of the foot, just for little short "drop" type passes. This would be when your team mate is maybe just 4-6 yards behind, and off to the side of you. Contact is usually made with inside of the foot. Lets say you are dribbling forward, and pushing the ball, with the instep of your right foot *(SEE FIGURE 39),* or any other foot for that matter. And then you want to make a drop pass, behind you,

FIGURE 39

to your right. What you would do is, switch the dribble to the outside of your right foot, slow down, almost stop the dribble, then take another short step with the left foot. Next you pivot on your left foot, turn, and kick the ball back to your team mate, using the inside of your left foot *(SEE FIGURE 40)*.

There is another way, to make the drop pass. As you are dribbling along with the right foot, (which is probably more common), you would slow down, let the ball almost stop, then swing the right foot around in front of the ball. Next you would kick the ball back, to the right, at an angle to your team mate, using

FIGURE 40

the outside rear heel of the right foot. To do this takes a backwards swinging motion, with the right foot. I don't recommend this though for 5-7 year olds, without several years of dribbling experience. It's not easy to do because you are kicking it back, almost blindly. However if you can master this technique, it will really fool your opponent, who will not be expecting it. Next reverse everything, and have them work on passing it back to the left.

Practice:

To practice the pivot and turn pass, find a large back yard, or field, to work on. Then have your son or daughter start dribbling slowly straight ahead. Before they start though mom or dad, you go about 5 -10 yards to the right side of them, and maybe just slightly back several yards. Then have them turn, pivot to their right, then pass you the ball with their left foot. After they have mastered turning and pivoting to their right, then have them work on turning, and pivoting to their left. When they turn to the left, they pass you the ball with their right foot. Even though one side or the other will be easier for them, teach them to pass to either side. Only after they have mastered the pivot and turn pass, then have them work on the rear heel blind pass, to both sides. Midfielders need to learn both of these techniques, and forwards probably could use this technique, to get the ball to other forwards, or strikers, coming up behind them attempting to score.

Drill No. 26- Hip Turn Pass

The Basics are:

Kicking the ball, with the instep part of the foot, has another not often used, special type of pass a player might use while running across the field laterally. This would be when you are moving across the field, and a high pass comes in to you, then suddenly you see a team mate break free into a clear area downfield, just before the pass gets to you. The team mate may not be open by the time you would turn, dribble, and go upfield to make the pass. So this is an option that can quickly get them the ball. Contact is made with the instep of the foot as you jump up and turn *(SEE FIGURE 41)*. This is a very hard pass to make because the jump up, and timing, has to be almost perfect. I would not even try this until your son or daughter has been playing, and kicking, for 3 or 4 years, and they are very athletic and coordinated. The key to making this pass is, knowing just which direction you want it to go, then watching it all the way into the foot for contact. Also the body has to be turned, just right so that the contact is made with the

STEP 1   STEP 2   STEP 3   STEP 4

FIGURE 41

instep, and not the inside part of the foot. The follow through goes right through the ball, then the kicking foot swings on around, and over towards, the non-kicking foot. This will help them to come down on their feet, and keep their balance *(SEE FIGURE 41)*.

Practice:

      To practice the hip turn pass, find a large back yard, or field, to work on. Then have your son or daughter start running slowly across the field. Before they start though mom or dad, take a ball and go to the opposite side of the field, straight ahead, and slightly back of the spot they are headed to. As they are approaching , and about 5 or 6 yards away from you, loft the ball up in the air, just high enough, so they can jump up and be able to meet the ball with their foot. This will probably take several tries, to get the timing down right with them. It's probably a good idea to walk, slowly through the movements, with them as to how they are going to jump up and turn. Also you might want to have them jump up, try a couple of fake kicks without the ball, just so they can get the feel of that part of the technique. I wouldn't worry about teaching this technique, to your son or daughter though until they get older.

Drill No. 27- Over the Head (Bicycle) Pass

The Basics are:

      Kicking the ball, with the instep part of the foot, has still another, not often used, special type of pass a player might be taking a high pass, and they want to kick behind them. This would be when you are moving away from the goal, and you know where your team mate is, behind you and ready to make a try for a goal. This is another option that can quickly get them the ball. Contact is made with the instep of the foot as you jump up, swing the kicking leg way up in the air, and catch the front part of the ball, at about head height *(SEE FIGURE 42)*. This is another very hard pass to make because the jump up, and timing, has to be almost perfect. I would not even try this until your son or daughter has been playing, and kicking, for at least 3 or 4 years, and they are very athletic and coordinated. The key to making this pass is, the timing and watching it, all the way onto the foot until contact is made. The follow through goes right through the ball, then the kicking foot swings on around until it is almost straight up. Then as you come down, you roll over towards the side of the non-kicking foot, and lightly break the fall with your arm *(SEE FIGURE 42)*. When they get older, they should learn to make this kick with both feet.

Practice:

To practice the over the head pass, find a large back yard, or field, to work on. Then have your son or daughter start running slowly towards you. Make sure they have some thick grass, or a soft spot, to land on while practicing this pass. Before they start though mom or dad, take a ball and go out straight ahead of them, and to a spot they are headed to. As they are approaching , and about 5 or 6 yards away from you, loft the ball up in the air, just high enough so they can jump up, and be able to meet the ball with the instep of their foot. This will probably take several tries, to get the ball timing down right, with them

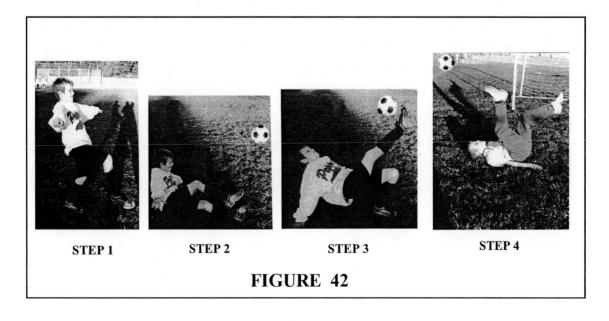

STEP 1   STEP 2   STEP 3   STEP 4

FIGURE 42

because it's very hard to do. It's probably a good idea, to first walk slowly through the movements with them as to how they are going to jump up, and kick up with their kicking foot. Also you might want to have them jump up, and try a couple of fake kicks without the ball, just so they can get the feel of that part of the technique. I wouldn't worry about teaching this technique to your son or daughter though until they get older. There are easier techniques they can use until then. Midfielders, forwards, and backs, might need to use this technique.

Drill No. 28- Overlap Run Pass

The Basics are:

The overlap run type of pass is a special type of tactical short pass. This is a pass, to fool an opponent, and get the ball upfield as quickly as possible. First the attacking player passes the ball to their team mate *(SEE FIGURE 43-A)*. The team mate then begins to dribble the ball, at an angle across the field, to their left. At that same time the attacking player swings around behind the team mate, in the opposite direction, to their right. Then as the attacking player has looped around the team mate, and is headed up the field, suddenly the team mate makes a short pass back to the attacking player, now moving up the field *(SEE FIGURE 43-B)*. The pass by the team mate is an inside of the foot type pass, which can be made very quickly, with the away (left) foot, right off the dribble.

A   B

FIGURE 43

Practice:

To practice the overlap run pass, find a large back yard, or field, to work on. Then have your son or daughter start slowly dribbling the ball diagonally across the field. Then you, mom or dad, go out in front, and to the left, of them a little bit. When they are about 5 or 6 yards away from you, they pass you the ball. Then you, mom or dad, start to dribble the ball away from them, slowly across the field. Give them a few seconds, to get looped back around and behind you. Next you, mom or dad, pivot and pass the ball back, and to your right, to them by kicking it with your left foot *(SEE FIGURE 43-B)*. Make sure to pass the ball, a yard or two, in front of them, so they don't have to stop running to receive the pass. Take turns with them on becoming the passer, and the attacker. This is so they can learn the moves of each player. Also practice this tactic moving the other way, which would be from left to the right. The key to this tactic is, making the pass back to the looping attacker. You have to be dribbling slowly, then as the right foot is pushing the ball ahead, you slow it down. Then you stop, plant the right foot, then pivot with it turn and make the kick, with the inside of the left foot. All of this will take lots of practice, to get the kick and the timing down. If they are a midfielder, or a back, they should learn both positions on this tactic. Even forwards could learn this tactic.

Drill No. 29- "Give and Go" Pass

The Basics are:

The "Give and Go" type of pass is, a special type of, tactical short pass. It is very similar to the "Overlap Run" pass. The difference is, it is more of a back and forth type play as two players move up the field, across from each other. This is another pass, to fool an opponent, and get the ball upfield as quickly as possible. First the attacking player passes the ball to their team mate *(SEE FIGURE 44-A)*. The team mate then begins to dribble the ball, straight ahead up the field. At that same time, the attacking player swings out to the right along with them up the field, at about 4 or 5 yards apart. Then as the attacking player gets up along side, and slightly ahead of them, then suddenly the team mate makes a short pass right back to the attacking player now moving up the field *(SEE FIGURE 44-B)*. The pass by the team mate is an inside of the foot type pass, which can be made very quickly with the away (left) foot, right off the dribble.

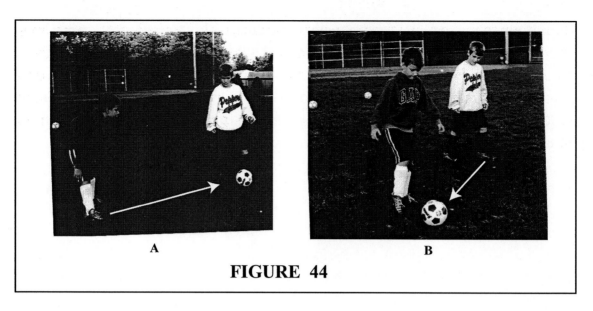

FIGURE 44

Practice:

To practice the "Give and Go" pass, find a large back yard, or field, to work on. Then have your son or daughter start slowly dribbling the ball straight up the field. Then you, mom or dad, go about 10 or 15 yards in front of them, and go slow waiting for the pass. As your son or daughter gets about 5 yards from you, they pass the ball to you, then they move up beside of you so you both are about 5 yards apart. While they are doing that, mom or dad, you slowly dribble the ball straight ahead. When they are almost up beside of you, give them a short inside of the left foot pass to the right of you *(SEE FIGURE 44-B)*, and just out in front of them. Then the two of you move down the field about 5 more yards then stop. Now go back and do it again, except this time your son or daughter comes up to the left (opposite from the other pass) of you. Then you make an inside of the foot pass, over to them, with the right foot. Have your son or daughter practice both, the attacker and the team mate, positions. And have them learn how to make the pass, first from one side, then the other. If they are a midfielder, or a back, they should learn both positions on this tactic. Even forwards could learn this tactic.

Drills for Ball Feel & Control

These drills are designed to improve their ability just to get the feel of the ball, control the ball, have quick reactions, and develop good concentration. Developing these skills, at an early age, will make them a much better soccer player later on. When a player learns how to control the ball instinctively, it

50

helps them to make plays they may not otherwise make. Ball control, sometimes referred to as "Juggling", really is just learning the art of getting the feel of it, and keeping the ball yourself. And all of this while keeping the opponent from taking the ball away from you. I might point out here that you ***can not*** use the arms, or hands, to control the ball. Basically there are 4 different techniques, to help train yourself to control the ball.

1. With the feet.
2. With the chest.
3. With the head.
4. With the thighs.

Drill No. 30- Juggling with the Feet

The Basics are:

Start by placing the ball on your instep *(SEE FIGURE 45)*. This is accomplished by tossing the ball in the air, and catching it on the instep. Or by placing the bottom of your foot on top of the ball, then rolling it backwards and slipping the foot underneath the ball while it rolls up on your instep *(SEE FIGURE 45)*. Next you lightly kick the ball up, with a quick flip of the ankle. Try to keep the ball from going up more than waist high. Then you just keep flipping the ball up and down *(SEE FIGURE 45)*, and catching it on the laces of the shoe. This is where it gets the name of "Juggling". The key to balancing the ball on the foot is, just as it comes down and contacts the foot, give a little with the foot by dropping it a little to absorb the downward impact.

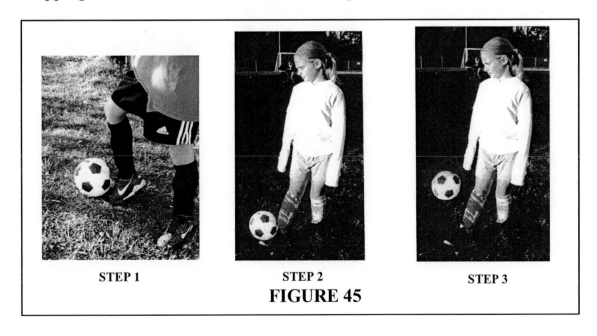

| STEP 1 | STEP 2 | STEP 3 |

FIGURE 45

Practice:

To practice juggling the ball with the foot, take your son or daughter out to the back yard on the grass. Have them use whichever, of the two ways, is the easiest for them to get the ball up on the shoe laces. Then have them flip the ball up and down. Tell them to see how long they can keep it in the air. You might also spice up the routine by saying, "Ill bet you can't keep it from hitting the ground for minute". Then if they can, take them out for an ice cream, or some type of treat. If they are having trouble though keep working with them until they master this technique. Repetition is the key here for success.

Drill No. 31- Topping with the Feet

The Basics are:

Start by standing right in front of the ball *(SEE FIGURE 46-A)*. Next in rapid succession they first place the bottom of the right foot on the top of the ball *(SEE FIGURE 46-B)*, then they quickly bring it back down to the starting position. After that they quickly place the bottom of the left foot on the top of the ball *(SEE FIGURE 46-C)*, Then quickly bring it back down to the starting position. What this ends up like is, a fast pumping up and down action of first one foot then the other, on the top of the ball. This is good practice for making quick stops while dribbling, backward passing, making the locomotive move, the maradona move, and the drag back turn move. It also programs their "muscle memory", and helps them improve on their foot quickness.

A   B   C

FIGURE 46

Practice:

To practice the topping drill, take your son or daughter out to the back yard on the grass. Have them stand stationary right in front of the ball. Then say "GO", and have them start pumping their feet up and down on the top of the ball. They should do this very fast for about 30 seconds, then holler "One" and stop and rest for about 1 minute. Then repeat for 30 seconds, and holler "Two". In other words they are counting the sets. Have them do at least 5 sets of these at a training session.

Drill No. 32- Side to Side with the Feet

The Basics are:

Start by standing with their feet spread way apart, and the ball placed on the inside of their left foot *(SEE FIGURE 47-A)*. Next they push or flick the ball over to the right foot, using the inside middle to front part of their left foot *(SEE FIGURE 47-B)*. Then using the same inside part of their right foot, they push or flick the ball back over to the left foot. Then while trying to remain in a stationary position, they keep the ball moving back and forth between each foot. Sometimes a little jumping hopping action helps keep

A   B

FIGURE 47

control of the ball. This is good practice for protecting the ball, making parallel side passes, and many of the trick moves. This drill also programs their "muscle memory", and helps them improve on their foot quickness.

Practice:

To practice the side to side drill, take your son or daughter out to the back yard on the grass. Have them stand with their feet way apart, and the ball next to the inside of their left foot. Then say "GO", and have them start slowly pushing the ball back and forth between each foot. As they get better at this drill they can try to speed it up a little. Have them try to stay as stationary as they can while doing this drill. They should do this as fast as they can for about 30 seconds, then holler "One" and stop and rest for about 1 minute. Then repeat for 30 seconds, and holler "Two". In other words they are counting the sets. Have them do at least 5 sets of these at a training session.

Drill No. 33- With the Chest

The Basics are:

Start by tossing the ball up in the air, then catching it on the chest *(SEE FIGURE 48).* The back has to be arched, otherwise the ball will just quickly slide down to the ground. The object is to control the ball, with the chest, then bouncing it down to the thigh and then down to the instep.

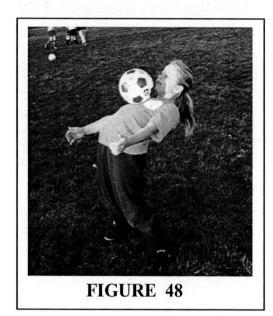

FIGURE 48

To practice juggling the ball, with the chest, take your son or daughter out to the back yard on the grass. Have them throw the ball up, then arch their back and bounce it off their chest, and then down to their thigh. Have them learn how to bounce it down to the left, or the right thigh. The reason is, if your opponent is coming in on your left, you want to bounce it down to the right thigh, to keep it as far away as possible from the approaching opponent. Then have them bounce it from the right thigh down to the right instep, then hold it there for control. Teach them to bounce it from the chest down to the left thigh, then also down to the left foot instep. This is for control on either side. If they are having trouble though, keep working with them until they master this technique. Repetition is the key here for success.

Drill No. 34- With the Head

The Basics are:

Start by tossing the ball up in the air, then catching it on the forehead about where the forehead meets the hair line *(SEE FIGURE 49)*. Or it may be easier to just place the ball on the fore head, and start from there. The object is to bounce the ball up and down on the forehead, without it falling to the ground.

Practice:

To practice juggling the ball with the head, take your son or daughter out to the back

FIGURE 49

yard on the grass. Have them throw, or place, the ball up on the forehead. Then have them flip the ball straight up in air, using a little spring upwards with the legs. Have them keep the neck bent back, so the bouncing ball always goes straight up. Have them juggle the ball up and down this way, for as long as they can. Do not use the very top of your head, or the face, to make contact. The key is to bounce it, with the neck bent back, and catch it every time right on the spot where the forehead and hairline meet. This way it bounces more straight up. Also don't let it bounce on the head while the head is still. Keep the knees bent and springy, and bend down a little just as it makes contact, to absorb to much upward force on the bounce. If they are having trouble though keep working with them until they master this technique. Repetition is the key here for success.

FIGURE 50

Drill No. 35- With the Thigh

The Basics are:

Start by tossing the ball up in the air, then catching it on the thigh *(SEE FIGURE 50)*. To catch the ball, bring the thigh up to about waist high. Bounce the ball up in the air, to about shoulder height. Do this by using little short up swinging motions with the leg. The object is to keep the ball bouncing off the knee, up and down, and going no higher than the shoulder. Once they have mastered the basic technique, probably with the dominant leg, then teach them to alternate from one thigh to the other and back again. This is really just a little juggling act using the thigh.

Practice:

To practice juggling the ball with the thighs, take your son or daughter out to the back yard on the grass. Have them throw the ball up in the air, then catch it on the thigh. Or it may be easier to start by just raising the thigh up, and placing the ball on it. Next have them flip the ball up in the air, using a little flip up with the leg. Then catch it, and flip it up again. Have them keep doing this, up and down, for as long as they can. Once they have mastered juggling the ball on one thigh, teach them to bounce it over to the other thigh, and juggle it there as long as they can. Last have them bounce it, back and forth, between thighs. If they are having trouble though keep working with them until they master this technique. Repetition is the key here for success.

Drills for Trapping and Receiving

Trapping or receiving the ball is very important in soccer because most of the time a player spends is either receiving passes, or trying to intercept them from the opposing team. Learning what to do without the ball is part of this. Players need to look for clear areas to receive passes, depending on where they need to be for a particular offensive strategy. Trapping and receiving the ball is where all of the ball control training comes in handy. This is because trapping and receiving is accomplished using the feet, chest, thighs, head, or by using the whole body. After learning how to control the ball *(SEE THE BALL CONTROL SECTION)*, each main technique has its own additional and special tactics, and techniques that go with it. One other thing I might point out is if you always keep your feet moving while attempting to trap or receive, it will allow you to make last minute adjustments. Lets start out with the feet because that's where trapping and receiving end up, down at the feet for passing.

Drill No. 36- Using the Feet

The Basics are:

The feet are probably the most common way players trap, or receive, the ball. The first thing your son or daughter has to learn how to do is, watch the ball

FIGURE 51

coming in and get in line with it so it's directly in front of you *(SEE FIGURE 51-A)*. Most players use the inside of the foot to control the incoming ball. How this is done is, use the inside of either foot to absorb the balls impact *(SEE FIGURE 51-B)*. It's probably better to use your dominant foot to do this. Mainly because your coordination will be better with that foot. You do this by relaxing the foot, so it can swing loosely and absorb the shock of the ball hitting it. Just as the ball hits let the foot move backwards, this will deaden the ball so that it does not bounce off your foot and away from you *(SEE FIGURE 51-C)*. Now the ball is right in front of you to start dribbling, or make a pass. There is another way to trap a high ball, or a bouncing incoming ball. That is by raising the foot way up in the air *(SEE FIGURE 52)*. I'm not recommending this for the little kids though because it's too hard for them to learn. They can learn how to do this when they are 12 years old, or older.

FIGURE 52

Practice:

To practice trapping or receiving the ball with the feet, take your son or daughter out to the back yard on the grass. Start them out by throwing the ball up in the air, towards them, from about 10 or 15 yards away. Have them get in front of the ball first, then trap it with their dominant foot. Next watch, and make sure they deaden the ball properly. The hardest part to teach them is going to be, deadening the ball as it hits their foot. If they do not learn how to do it correctly, the ball will probably take a big bounce off their foot, and away from them. If they can not seem to learn how to do this, you will have to get up real close to them with an easy throw. Before the throw, go over in slow motion with them, showing them the motions the foot will have to take. Then have them put the whole technique together, but this time using real easy under hand throws to them. Keep doing this with them until they can master it. They can learn how to do this, you will just have to go through it with them over and over. Midfielders, backs, defenders, and forwards must learn this skill.

Drill No. 37- With the Chest or the Whole Body

The Basics are:

Trapping or receiving the ball with the chest *(SEE FIGURE 53-A)*, or the whole body *(SEE FIGURE 53-B)*, is probably the second best or most common way to trap the ball. I suspect with the little kids, it will be the best way to trap a high, or bouncing, incoming ball. Much easier fir them to learn than using the "raising the foot technique" to stop it. However, little kids have to be careful with their timing, and coordination, and not to let it hit them in the face. So make sure you talk to them first about this technique, and warn them of it's danger.

To keep it from hitting their face, show them how to tilt the neck, and head

A   B

FIGURE 53

back, and let it hit the chest area. To explain this to them, I would stand just to the side of them and slowly with an open palm, move my hand in front of them following the imaginary flight of the incoming ball into their chest. And in slow motion as your hand comes in, they have to tilt their neck and head back. Then little by little speed up your hand. They in turn have to speed up, keep focused, and judge when to tilt the neck and head back. The key to this is the timing, and being in just the right place as the ball comes down.

Practice:

To practice this, start out by taking your son or daughter out to the back yard. Then you, mom or dad, go out first about 5 yards away from them, and have them face you. Next make an underhand lob throw into them. First have them try to receive it on the chest *(SEE FIGURE 53-A)*, deaden it by moving slightly backwards, then letting it fall right in front of them. Now they are ready to start dribbling with it, or in this case make an inside of the foot pass back to you. Next make a short underhand lob throw into them, and have them receive it using the whole body *(SEE FIGURE 53-B)*. They do this by arching their back, throw their arms back, and just let the ball hit their chest. Then just as it hits their chest, they move slightly back to deaden the balls impact. After that they let the ball roll down to the ground. Now they are ready again to start dribbling with it, or again in this case make an inside of the foot pass back to you. It will probably take a lot of short practice throws, over and over again, for them to learn how to do this. All players need to learn this, especially sweepers, fullbacks, and defenders.

Drill No. 38- With the Thighs

The Basics are:

Trapping or receiving the ball, with the thighs, is really just the next step after receiving it with the chest. If you try to trap the ball directly on the thigh, it is much more difficult to deaden it. What is probably going to happen with kids is, the ball will bounce hard off the thigh, and away from them. This could result in giving the opposing team a chance, to gain control of the ball. It is probably easier to trap the ball on short passes, or kicks, in the air. However, on long passes or kicks in the air, the probability is it will bounce off very hard. So what this means is, go with the chest trap first because there is less chance of error. Wait until they are 12 years, or older, to practice this technique.

Practice:

Wait until they are 12 years or older to practice this technique. Because at that age, they will understand better how to learn this technique.

Drill No. 39- With the Head

The Basics are:

Trapping or receiving the ball with the head is possible, but really very hard to accomplish. As with trapping with the thighs, trapping with the head has an even higher probability of bouncing off very hard, especially with long passes or kicks in the air. This is because the ball is coming in really hard, making it very difficult to deaden. It may be easier to trap or receive the ball on short passes, or kicks in the air. However, on long passes or kicks in the air, the probability is it will bounce off very hard. So what this means is, go with the chest trap first because there is less chance of error.

FIGURE 54

Practice:

Wait until they are 12 years or older to practice this technique. Because at that age, they will understand better how to learn this technique.

FIGURE 55

Drills for Throwing

Throwing with the hands is very limited in soccer. Only "goalkeepers", and players making a "Throw In" when the ball goes out of play, can use their hands. And the "goalkeeper" is limited to using their hands, only within the penalty area. It is a rule that the "Thrower" can not make a play, after throwing in the ball, until another player has touched the ball. Another rule is, you can not score a goal directly from a "Throw in". There are basic techniques for goalkeepers, and throw in thrower's. Since "goalkeepers" are such a very important part of the game of soccer, we will start with them first.

FIGURE 56

Drill No. 40- Goalkeepers Throwing

The Basics are:

The "goalkeeper" can throw, or roll, the ball out to a team mate as a method of distributing the ball after he has made a save. Sometimes a long accurate throw out to a defender can be more effective than a kick. When they throw the ball, the "goalkeeper" can use three different methods for a throw.

1. Two arm overhead throw *(SEE FIGURE 54).*
2. One hand side arm throw *(SEE FIGURE 55).*
3. One hand overhead throw *(SEE FIGURE 56).*

FIGURE 57

The two arm overhead throw can be effective for shorter throws, out to a team mate. This is usually accomplished, by grabbing the ball with both hands over the head, then taking a short 2 or 3 step run up to the release point. Holding the ball with the fingers, in a diamond grip, is the most common way *(SEE FIGURE 57).* As you make the release, you should throw off of the dominant or strong foot. That is, plant that foot slightly out in front, bend the knees slightly, let go of the ball with a snapping action of the arms and body.

The one hand side arm throw can be effective for the intermediate, and longer throws. This is accomplished, by grabbing the ball, with your dominant or strong arm. The ball is gripped for release, by hooking the hand and wrist around the ball *(SEE FIGURE 58).* To make the throw, first grab the ball with both hands to steady it, then take a 2 or 3 step run up to the release point. To release the ball, plant the foot on the non throwing hand side out in front, bend the knees, bring the ball back with both

FIGURE 58

hands. Then let go, with the non throwing hand as the arm whips around forward to make the throw.

The overhand throw is for longer more accurate throws. It is probably more accurate than the side arm throw. However, I don't recommend this for the real little kids because their hands are too small to palm, or grip, the ball. This is a very good technique though if your son or daughter can hold onto the ball. This throw is accomplished by grabbing the ball, with both hands to steady it, then take a 2 or 3 step run up to the release point. To release the ball, plant the foot on the non throwing hand side out in front, bend the knees, and bring the ball back with both hands. Then let go with the non throwing hand as the arm snaps forward over the head to make the throw.

Practice:

For "goalkeepers" to practice these throws, find a large backyard or a grassy park area. Give your son or daughter the ball, go out about 10 yards away from them, and have them first try the two handed throw. Make sure their technique is correct, and they get the ball to you aiming about chest height. After a few tries, have them get the ball to you on a low bounce, so you can stop it and control it with your foot.

Next move out to about 15 yards away, and have them try the side arm pass. First at about chest height, then on a low bounce, so you can stop it and control it with your foot. This is probably going to be the easiest one for them to use. And it will be a throw they get out to you at the longer distances. The problem if they have one, is going to be the accuracy of their throws. Keep working with them until they master this technique accurately.

Last have them try the overhand throw. If their hand is to small, to properly hold onto the ball, then don't worry about teaching them this technique until they get older. If they can hold onto

FIGURE 59

the ball, have them try this throw to you. Again first to the chest, then on a low bounce to you.

Drill No. 41- Side Line Throw In

The Basics are:

    The side line "Throw in" must be made with two hands from behind, and over the head, and the feet must be on the ground. At the time of ball release, the feet can be on the line or outside of the line. They *can not* be inside of the line. This is usually accomplished, by grabbing the ball, with both hands over the head. Then taking a short 2 or 3 step run up to the release point. Holding the ball with a diamond grip is the most common way *(SEE FIGURE 57)*. The diamond is formed by the thumbs and forefingers, forming the diamond shape. As you make the release, you should throw off of the dominant or strong foot. That is, plant that foot slightly out in front, and bend the knees. Any player, except the goalkeeper, can make the throw in.

  Practice:

    For "Throw In" players to practice these throws, find a large backyard or a grassy park area. You may also have to bring a long strip of 5 inch wide white cloth with you, to simulate the side line. Then weight it down with old white plastic milk bottles filled with sand, kitty litter, or water. Give your son or daughter the ball, then go out about 10 yards away from them. Then have them get behind the touch line, and make the short run up two handed pass to you. Make sure their technique is correct, and they get the ball to you aiming about chest height. After a few tries, have them get the ball to you on a low bounce, so you can stop it and control it with your foot.

FIGURE 60

    Also work with them on getting as close to the touch line as possible, without going over it into the field as they make their ball release. And observe that they have both feet on the ground at the point of release. You can be up on your toes though *(SEE FIGURE 59)*. Another trick to the "throw in" is, arch the back just as you start to move the arms forward *(SEE FIGURE 60)*. Throwing off the strong or dominant foot with a whip like snapping action, will put some power to the throws. This is important when you have to make long throws. For longer throws, mom or dad, you want to go out to about 15 yards away.

All players, except the "goalkeeper", need to learn this particular throwing skill. This is because who ever is near the point on the side line where the ball went out of bounds, has to go out and make the throw in. The game can not be held up while the coach finds a specialist to run in, and make the "Throw in", as happens in some of the other sports.

Drills for Heading

Heading the ball is one of the more difficult techniques for young kids to learn. Some authorities say, don't let little kids head the ball at all. They say it's too dangerous. I think it may be allright for ball control (juggling) drills, but if your son or daughter does not need to use this technique until they get older, then why take the chance. The timing has be nearly perfect anyway, or you might miss the ball altogether with the head. Remember now I'm talking about long incoming balls up in the air. Also if your young son or daughter is afraid of heading the ball, don't force them to try it.

And if you do start teaching them to head the ball, then limit the number of times they practice it, at any given practice session, to reduce the possibility of injury. See the chapter on "Ball Control", for the correct way to make contact with the head. My suggestion is to wait until they are 12 years, or older, to even try to teach them this technique.

Drills for Tackling

In soccer, tackling is a method by which the defense tries to regain control of the ball. When they talk about "tackling", almost everyone thinks of the slide tackle. However there are other ways to make a tackle. They are, ground tackles, head on tackles, side tackles, shoulder tackles, and hook tackles. To be good at tackling, the defensive player needs to anticipate what the opponent is going to do. Which technique to use, is going to depend upon where you are in relation to the opponent. In front, behind, to the side, and how fast they are running. The thing to remember with "tackling" is, after the tackle, you have to get control of the ball and go on the attack. Except for the "slide or hook tackle", it's best to remain on you feet. If you fall down, the opponent is probably going to get away.

By remaining on your feet you may get a second, or third, chance to gain control of the ball. Lets start out with Tackling techniques where you stay on your feet because they are easier to learn.

Drill No. 42- The Ground Tackle

The Basics are:

This may be one of the easiest tackles to make when the opponent is coming in head on into your son or daughter. This tackle gets it's name because the ball is rolling on the ground. When the opponent is dribbling the ball right at them, and very close, they need to do two things. The first one is, they line up their foot on the same side the dribblers foot is on *(SEE FIGURE 61-A)*. The second thing is, watch the ball and not the players eyes. This way they won't get faked out. Next as the opponents dribble leg moves forward, your son or daughter swings their foot at the ball and meets it with the inside of their foot *(SEE FIGURE 61-B)*. After contact is made, they have to keep pressure on the ball, by pushing and tensing up their leg. Also remind them that they must go for the ball first, and not kick the opponents leg. Then they need to try to roll the ball away from the opponent, by flicking it back between the opponents legs, to get control.

A   B

FIGURE 61

Practice:

To practice this technique, mom or dad you take the ball, and have your son or daughter go out straight in front of you about 3 or 4 yards. Then you slowly dribble the ball straight ahead. As you start to dribble, you son or daughter slowly runs right at you. When they get about a yard or two away, have them match their leg up with whichever leg you are dribbling with, and watch the ball. Next they swing the inside of their foot right up against the ball, tense their leg, push, and keep pressure on the ball. Then have them quickly try to roll the ball away from you. If they are using their left foot to make contact, then they should roll the ball to the right, through your legs and behind you. If they are blocking with the right foot, they should roll the ball to the left and through your legs. Make sure they practice blocking with either foot. Defenders, midfielders, and backs, should learn this technique.

Drill No. 43- The Head On Tackle

The Basics are:

The head on tackle is really just "Intercepting" a pass to an opponent by running right in front of them, stopping , and controlling the ball with the inside of their foot. It gets it's name from running "head on" into the ball, right in front

FIGURE 62

of the opponent. To do this your son or daughter needs to get into position, sort of diagonally behind the opponent as they are waiting for the ball to come to the opponent. As they see the ball coming , they start to take little short choppy steps, and head around and in front of the opponent, just before they get the ball *(SEE FIGURE 62)*. They need to use their body, to hold the position in front of the opponent, then use the inside of their foot to stop, and move the ball away from the opponent. This is a timing play. You will have to work with your son or daughter, to teach them just how far away they need to be behind you, to make their move in front of you for the ball .

Practice:

To practice this technique mom or dad, you will need 3 people. You, mom or dad, act as the player receiving the pass. Have your son or daughter get diagonally behind you, about 2 or 3 yards away to your left rear. Have the third person with the ball, go out to a spot about 10 or 12 yards in front of you. Then have that person kick the ball to you on the ground. As soon as the ball is kicked, your son or daughter starts moving forward, taking short choppy steps. When the ball is almost to you, your son or daughter breaks around in front of you, and blocks you off with their body. Next they stop the ball, with the inside of their foot, and deflect it off to the side and away from you. Have them switch, then come from your right rear, and make the play. Next have them execute the stop, and deflect or control the ball, using either foot. Defenders, midfielders, and backs, should learn this technique.

Drill No. 44- The Side Tackle

The Basics are:

This may be one of the easiest tackles to make when the opponent is running along side of or near your son or daughter, and while dribbling the ball *(SEE FIGURE 63-A)*. This tackle gets it's name because your son or daughter has positioned themselves right along side of the opponent. As the opponent is dribbling the ball, and they attempt to kick a pass, your son or daughter comes in swings their leg in front of the ball and attempts to block or deflect it with either the inside or outside of their foot *(SEE FIGURE 63-B)*. If they can, they want to block the ball with one foot, and steal it away with the other foot. As an example while running along the right hand side of an opponent, who is dribbling the ball with their right foot, you would speed up and get slightly ahead of them. Then suddenly you would swing your left foot in front of the ball. Using the outside

A   B

FIGURE 63

of the left foot to block and stop the ball, then keeping pressure on it, try to roll it away back towards you. If you succeed, then you would quickly swing the right foot around, and control the ball with the inside of the right foot. Also if the opponent is dribbling with their left foot it is more advantageous to come up on the opponents left side, and block with the right foot. Once you get close to the opponent the key is, keep your eyes on the ball.

Practice:

To practice this technique mom or dad, take the ball and go out to an open space in your yard. Start to dribble the ball slowly with your right foot. Have your son or daughter get 1 or 2 yards away from you, on your right side. As you are running and dribbling, and they are side by side with you, have them suddenly and quickly speed up a little ahead of you, then swing the outside of their left foot in front of the ball and stop or block it. You will probably want to walk through this slowly with them, to get their footwork right. After they have blocked the ball, have them keep pressure on it by stiffening their leg. Next they try to roll the ball back towards them, still using the left foot. If they can roll the ball away from your foot, then they would turn, pivot, and swing the right foot around, so they can dribble the ball away with the inside of the right foot. Have them work this technique from your left side also, using the outside of their right foot to block the ball. Have them next attempt to roll the ball away with the right foot, then dribble it away with the inside of their left foot. Defenders, midfielders, and backs, should learn this technique.

Drill No. 45- The Shoulder Tackle

The Basics are:

The shoulder tackle is another tackle where your son or daughter is running along side of, and touching the shoulder of, the opponent who is waiting for the pass on the ground *(SEE FIGURE 64-A)*. This tackle gets it's name because the

| A | B | C | D |

FIGURE 64

players are touching shoulders. However each player must keep their elbows close to the body, and be in the act of going for the ball, otherwise a pushing foul may be called. And this touching of shoulders can only occur when the ball is very close to the players. The next move is, swinging the right shoulder and right leg around to block off the opponent, then using the outside of the left foot to stop the ball, and deflect it away from the opponent *(SEE FIGURE 64-B)*. That move is followed by pivoting and turning around to the left, letting the opponent go on by, then looking for the ball *(SEE FIGURE 64-C)*. Once they see where the ball is, they go to it and start dribbling with the inside of the right foot, or pass it to a team mate *(SEE FIGURE 64-D)*.

Practice:

To practice this technique mom or dad, you will need 3 people. You, mom or dad, act as the player receiving the pass. Have your son or daughter get beside you, about 1 or 2 yards away, on your left. Have the third person with the ball, go out to a spot about 10 or 12 yards in front of you Then have that person kick the ball to you on the ground, as both of you slowly start to run forward. As soon as the ball is kicked your son or daughter starts moving up, next to you, and lightly touches your left shoulder. Then as both of you move ahead towards the incoming ball, have your son or daughter suddenly move quickly just ahead of you, and block you off with their right shoulder *(SEE FIGURE 64-A)*. Next they stop the ball with the outside of their left foot, and deflect it to their left away from you *(SEE FIGURE 64-B)*. Their next move is to keep you blocked off as they pivot, turn *(SEE FIGURE 64-C)*, then swing the right foot around to their right, and move to control the ball with the inside of their right foot *(SEE FIGURE 64-D)*. After they master the technique from the left side of you, then have them come up on your right side, and block the ball with the outside of their right foot. Defenders, midfielders, backs, and even forwards, should learn this technique.

Drill No. 46- The Slide Tackle

The Basics are:

The "Slide Tackle" is one of the more popular, and exciting, tackles because when it is done right, it can be very spectacular. It gets it's name from the body sliding around in front of the opponent, to block the ball. However, it's not a very easy technique for young kids, to learn. This situation develops when a dribbling opponent has broken away from you, and you are trying to catch up to them from behind *(SEE FIGURE 65-A)*. What the defender has to do then is accelerate, then make a strong leg swinging slide out in front of the dribbler, to block the ball *(SEE FIGURE 65-B)*. The slide has to be made by rolling over on your side, so you can cross over and make the block with the outside leg *(SEE FIGURE 65-C)*. When contact with the ball is made, the defender has to complete the play by kicking the ball away from the attacker causing them to lose control *(SEE FIGURE 65-D)*. This is another timing play. You *can not* make contact with the opponents leg before making contact with the ball, or a foul will be called. Keeping your eyes on the ball, all the way through from slide to contact, is very important. The disadvantage of this technique is, if your timing is bad and you miss the ball, you are probably down on the ground, and out of any continuation of this play. Do not try to use this technique until you have been practicing it for several years, or you are 12 years or older.

Practice:

To practice this technique mom or dad, you go out in the back yard to a soft grassy area, or in the park. Take the ball and start dribbling slowly straight ahead. Have your son or daughter come up from behind you, about 1 or 2 yards away, on your left *(SEE FIGURE 65-A)*. When they get about even with you they start their slide, by dropping down, rolling to the right, and tucking in the right leg *(SEE FIGURE 65-B)*. Next, as they hit the ground sliding, the right leg should be tucked in, and the left leg then swings over and out in front of the ball

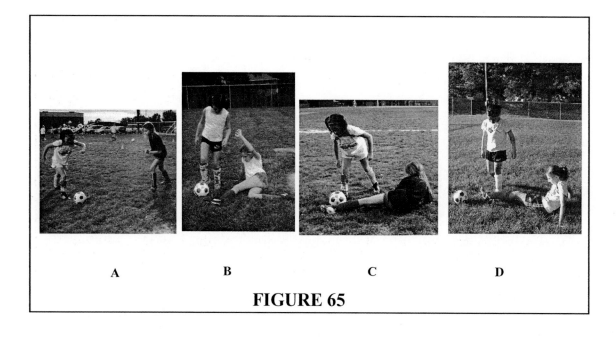

A	B	C	D

FIGURE 65

to make contact *(SEE FIGURE 65-C)*. Have them be careful that they contact the ball, *and not* your leg. If they contact the ball first, and then your leg, it *is not* a foul. When they make contact, the ball should be kicked away using the instep, or bottom, part of the left foot *(SEE FIGURE 65-D)*.

The key to making this technique work is, accelerating very fast so that the slide is fast enough to get them out in front of the dribbling opponent. When they have mastered the "Slide" technique from your left side, then have them reverse everything, and practice it from your right side. Defenders, midfielders, backs, and all attacking players, should learn this technique.

Drill No. 47- The Hook Tackle

The Basics are:

The Hook tackle is similar to the "ground tackle", except your son or daughter is coming straight at the dribbling opponent *(SEE FIGURE 66-A)*. It gets it's name from the going down, and hooking the leg around, to block the ball. When the opponent is dribbling the ball right at them, and very close, they need to do two things. The first one is, they slow down, and square away right in front of the dribbling opponent *(SEE FIGURE 66-A)*. The second one is, they check which direction the opponent is going to dribble *(SEE FIGURE 66-B)*. Next they they get into position to go down into a slide, towards the side the dribbler turns to, and make a hook block *(SEE FIGURE 66-C)*. After making

A   B   C   D

FIGURE 66

contact, the defender goes into a slide to try and roll or push the ball away from the dribbler, or push it over to a nearby team mate *(SEE FIGURE 66-D)*.

Practice:

To practice this technique mom or dad, you take the ball, and have your son or daughter go out straight in front of you about 3 or 4 yards. Then you slowly dribble the ball straight ahead. As you start to dribble, your son or daughter slowly runs right at you. When they get about a yard or two away, they spread their feet apart, the arms go out to their sides for balance in a wait and see position *(SEE FIGURE 66-A)*. *With* their arms out at their sides for balance, they can shift to either side very quickly. Next they have to determine which side you are going to try and get around them on. Lets say you, mom or dad, try to go around them to your right (their Left). They would then pivot to their left on their right foot, then take a little stutter step with the right foot *(SEE FIGURE 66-B)*. Then they get ready to go down into a slide, by tucking the right leg in, then hook blocking the ball with the left leg *(SEE FIGURE 66-C)*. After that they go into their slide, put the right hand down on the ground, the left arm out for balance, and roll the ball with their left leg pushing it away *(SEE FIGURE 66-D)*. After they have mastered the technique, going to their left, then reverse everything and have them practice the technique going to their right. Defenders, midfielders, and backs, should learn this technique.

Drills for Blocking and Stealing

The Basics are:

Blocking and stealing, in soccer, is just what says it is. "Blocking" is getting in front of a kick, or passed ball, and keeping it from going to an opposing player, or through the goal post to score a goal. And "Stealing" the ball means after you block the ball, you take control and go on offense, then either dribble or pass the ball towards your own goal. Both of these are Defensive Tactics. The skills for "Blocking" can be found in the sections on "BALL CONTROL", and "TRAPPING AND RECEIVING". The skills for "Wall Blocking", on free kicks, can be found in the section on "KICKING AND SHOOTING". The skills for "Stealing" can be found in the section on "TACKLING".

Practice:

To practice these skills, go to the sections mentioned, work on the drills that either stop the ball in the air or on the ground, or take it away from the opposing player dribbling or attempting to receive the ball. Defenders, midfielders, and backs, should learn these techniques.

Drills for Faking and Tricking

Learning how to fake, and trick, your opponent in soccer can sometimes really "Level the Playing Field", so to speak. There are times when you can over power your opponent. And then there are times when your opponent is bigger, and they are over powering you. That is the time you need an edge. These drills will give you an edge, especially if your son or daughter start to work on them when they are 5 or 6 years old. Some of these techniques are going to be very difficult for them to learn. However if you work with them on these drills when they are bored, or can't think of what to do at home, they will eventually begin to learn by doing them over, and over, and over. Repetition will become a habit. Some of these techniques are named after famous soccer players that developed them, or use them all the time.

There are many ways to fake an opponent. Changing directions, Zig Zagging to get your opponents feet all tangled up, and moving and shaking the head from side to side. There are some moves, and techniques, that only star players just naturally seem to know. We can not cover all of the possible moves, but we will cover some of the more common moves players make. Fakes, and tricks, break down into basically four categories:
1. Change of Speed Fakes.
2. Looking Fakes.
3. Body and Foot Fakes.
4. Passing and Shooting Fakes.

Change of Speed Fakes

Drill No. 48- The Slow and Go

The Basics are:
The technique here is, the player dribbling the ball "slows" way down as an opposing player approaches. This causes the approaching player to slow down also. Then suddenly, as the player does slow down in front of you, speed up very quickly and "go" around and away from them. This will not work for many players because they are too slow with their feet. However if your son or daughter can accelerate, and dribble fast, it can be an effective move for them.

A   B   C

FIGURE 67

Practice:

To practice this technique, go out to a big back yard or a park area, and you mom or dad go to a spot about 8 or 10 yards out in front of your son or daughter. Have them start dribbling the ball towards you, then you start running right at them. When you, mom or dad, get 3 yards away from them then have them slow down almost to a stop *(SEE FIGURE 67-A)*. Then you slow down also. Just as you slow down, they suddenly start dribbling the ball at an angle to the right, away from you as fast as they can, starting with the outside of their right foot *(SEE FIGURE 67-B)*. Since they need the practice, make a feeble effort to stop them, then let them get away *(SEE FIGURE 67-C)*. Have them work on this play, by sprint dribbling first to one side then the other. Defenders, midfielders, backs, and all attacking players, should learn this technique.

Drill No. 49- The Locomotive (or Leo)

The Basics are:

The technique here is the player dribbling the ball pretends to "stop" as an opposing player approaches, just to throw off the defense. This action can cause the approaching player to slow down, or it may draw the defense over to you, and open up an area somewhere else for passing the ball. This can be a little tricky, and harder to learn for the little kids, but it can work for players 12 years,

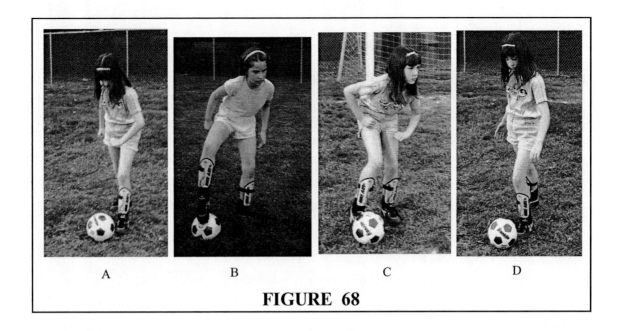

A   B   C   D

FIGURE 68

and older. The reason is, if you draw several players towards you, they have a good chance of taking the ball away from you. And also it will be harder for little kids to loft the ball over the heads of the several approaching players.

Practice:

To practice this technique, go out to a big back yard or a park area, and you mom or dad go to a spot about 8 or 10 yards out in front of your son or daughter. Have them start dribbling the ball towards you *(SEE FIGURE 68-A)*, then you start running slowly right at them . When you, mom or dad, get 5 yards away from them, have them bring up the right foot over the top of the ball, and fake a stop with the sole of the shoe *(SEE FIGURE 68-B).* But what they are really going to do is, just slow the ball down a bit using the sole of the right foot. Next have them bring the right foot down and back behind the ball *(SEE FIG-URE 68-C),* and pretend to go to the left. Then quickly they swing the left foot over and start to dribble away from you to their right, using the inside of the left foot *(SEE FIGURE 68-D)*. When they have mastered this move with the right foot, have them try the other side. Then if they can, practice reversing everything, and try this move using the left foot to slow the ball down. Defenders, midfielders, backs, and all attacking players, should learn this technique.

Looking Fakes

Drill No. 50- Head and Eye Fakes

The Basics are:

The technique with this fake is, the dribbler looks in one direction with the head and eyes, then goes in the opposite direction for a quick break away. How this works is, you get the opposing player to lean, or start to go, in the direction you are looking. And then you slow the ball down and with a quick jab step, you pivot, turn, then you push off hard and go in the other direction. Even if your son or daughter is not very fast if they can get the opposing player to commit in the direction they are looking to just before the player gets to them, this will work for them. Then next make the jab step in that direction, and then there is a good chance you can successfully make the break away in the other direction. To really sell the opposing player on the fake, you have to teach your son or daughter to look intensely in the fake direction. You will also have to teach them to accelerate, very fast, after the jab step though in order to get away without being intercepted.

Practice:

To practice this technique, go out to a big back yard or a park area, and you mom or dad go to a spot about 6 or 8 yards out in front of your son or

A   B   C

FIGURE 69

daughter. Have them start dribbling the ball towards you *(SEE FIGURE 69-A)*, then you start running slowly right at them. When you, mom or dad, get 3 yards away from them, have them slow down almost to a stop. Then you, mom or dad, pretend to get faked into leaning, then going to your right *(SEE FIGURE 69-B)*. Next have your son or daughter do a jab step to their left, then swing and roll the left foot over the top of the ball making it go right *(SEE FIGURE 69-B)*. Then they change dribble direction and dribble off to their right, starting with the inside of the left foot. And since they are the one needing the practice, then you mom or dad let them get away, around you, to your left *(SEE FIGURE 69-C)*. After they have mastered the play around to your left, then reverse everything and have them practice getting away, around to your right. Defenders, midfielders, backs, and all attacking players should learn this technique.

<u>Body and Foot Fakes</u>

Drill No. 51- Quick Feet Direction Change

The Basics are:

    This technique is really just a quick feet move, to change direction very suddenly. When an opponent is coming up on you, this could make them think you are going left when you wanted to go the right all along. As in most of the fake moves, this will be hard for the younger kids to learn. When they are 5 or 6

| A | B | C | D |

FIGURE 70

years old, their foot coordination is not too good. Their feet seem to get tangled up real easy on moves like this. Which means this technique is probably better suited for kids 12 years, and older. Generally how it works is, the dribbling player is dribbling in one direction, then swings one foot over the ball straddling it, and next pivots on the swing over leg, then dribbles in the other direction with the other foot.

Practice:

To practice this technique, go out to a big back yard or a park area, and give your son or daughter the ball. Have them go out about 10 yards in front of you. Then have them start to dribble straight ahead, slowly at first, using the right foot. Then have them lean a little bit to their left *(SEE FIGURE 70-A)*. Next they swing the left foot over the ball, so they are almost straddling it *(SEE FIGURE 70-B)*. After that they pivot on the swing over foot, and shift their weight, so they are starting to lean and go to their right *(SEE FIGURE 70-C)*. Then have them push off with the left pivot foot, and start dribbling to their right using the outside of their right foot *(SEE FIGURE 70-D)*. Once they have mastered faking left and going right, then reverse everything and have them try faking right and going left. They need to learn how to go either way. It's going to depend on where the opposing players are, in relation to them. Defenders, midfielders, backs, and all attacking players, should learn this technique.

Drill No. 52- The Maradona Move

A   B   C   D

FIGURE 71

The Basics are:

This move is named after the famous "Argentine" soccer player, Diego Maradona. How this works is when a pass or a kicked ball comes close, you stop the ball with the top of your right foot. Then you step off, and back, of the ball. Next turn your body to face in the opposite direction, of where you really want to go. Next you drag the ball backwards with your left foot, then quickly turn all the way around and dribble the ball in the opposite direction, which is where you really wanted to go all along. This all has to be accomplished very quickly, or an opposing team player may come up and steal the ball away. This move will be very difficult for younger kids to learn. You can try it with them, but you may have to wait until they are 12 years, or older.

Practice:

To practice this technique, go out to a big back yard or a park area, and you mom or dad go to a spot about 5 or 10 yards out in front of your son or daughter. Next take the ball and roll it to them. When the ball gets close, have them stop the ball, using the sole of their right foot *(SEE FIGURE 71-A)* over the top of the ball. Then have them step back off the ball, with their right foot just behind, and to the right of, the ball. Next they take a quick short step back with their left foot, turn and swing the right foot way out so they are straddling the ball and facing left *(SEE FIGURE 71-B)*. After that they drag the sole of the left foot over the top of the ball, making it go backwards a little bit, and clear of the left foot *(SEE FIGURE 71-C)*. Once the ball has cleared the left foot, they pivot all the way around with the left foot, then swing the right foot all the way around in back so they are facing to the right *(SEE FIGURE 71-D)*. Now they are ready dribble the ball in the direction (right) they really wanted to go in, using the inside of the right foot. When they have mastered this move with the right foot, you can try to reverse everything and have them practice stopping the ball with their left foot. Defenders, midfielders, backs, and all attacking players, should learn this technique.

Passing and Shooting Fakes

Drill No. 53- The Drag Back Turn

The Basics are:

This is a kicking fake move. How this works is you pretend to kick the ball , by planting the left foot, and bringing the right foot back as if to kick the ball. Then you swing the right foot over the top of the ball, and on the back swing you catch the top of the ball with the sole of the right foot, and roll it backwards. Next you pivot on your non-kicking foot, turn towards the direction you want to go, and dribble away from the opposing player. This all has to accomplished

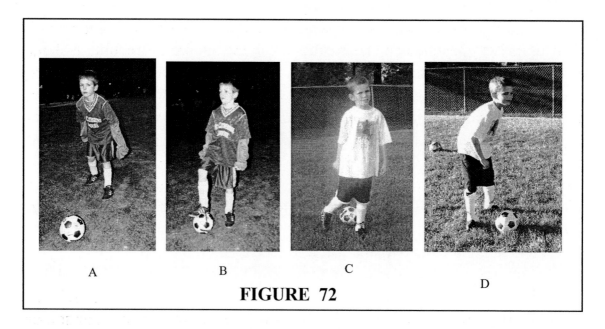

A   B   C   D

FIGURE 72

very quickly, or an opposing team player may come up and steal the ball away. This move will also be difficult for the younger kids to learn. You can try it with them, but you may have to wait until they are 12 years, or older.

Practice:

To practice this technique, go out to a big back yard or a park area, and you mom or dad go to a spot about 8 or 10 yards out in front of your son or daughter. Give them the ball, and have them start to dribble slowly ahead. Then you, mom or dad, start to run slowly at them. When they see that you are approaching them, have them pretend to kick the ball with their right foot *(SEE FIGURE 72-A)*. They don't kick the ball though. Instead they swing over the top of the ball with the right foot. On the back swing of the right foot they drag the sole of the shoe over the top of the ball making it roll backwards a little bit *(SEE FIGURE 72-B)*. When it gets behind the non-kicking leg *(SEE FIGURE 72-C),* they step on out in front with the right foot, pivot on it, turn to the left, and swing the left foot around behind the ball *(SEE FIGURE 72-D)*. And last when they are completely turned around, they dribble off to their left using the left foot. When they have mastered this move, with the right foot, you can try to reverse everything and have them practice faking the kick with their left foot.

Defenders, midfielders, backs, and all attacking players, should learn this technique.

Drill No. 54- The Cruyff Turn

The Basics are:

This is another kicking fake move very similar to the "Drag back turn". This move is named after the famous Dutch soccer player, Johan Cruyff. How this works is you pretend to kick the ball, by planting the left foot, and bringing the right foot back as if to kick the ball. But don't kick the ball. Instead you swing the right foot around to the right side of the ball. Then when the right foot comes down, lean forward on the left leg and use your right foot to push the ball behind and to your left. Next pivot on your right foot, turn to your left, and start dribbling off to your left, using the outside of the left foot. This move will also be very difficult for the younger kids to learn. You can try it with them, but you may have to wait until they are 12 years, or older.

Practice:

To practice this technique, go out to a big back yard or a park area, Then you, mom or dad, go to a spot about 8 or 10 yards out in front of your son or daughter. Give them the ball and have them start to dribble slowly ahead. Then you, mom or dad, start to run slowly at them. When they see you are approaching them, have them pretend to kick the ball with their right foot *(SEE FIGURE 73-A)*. They don't kick the ball though. Instead they swing the right foot

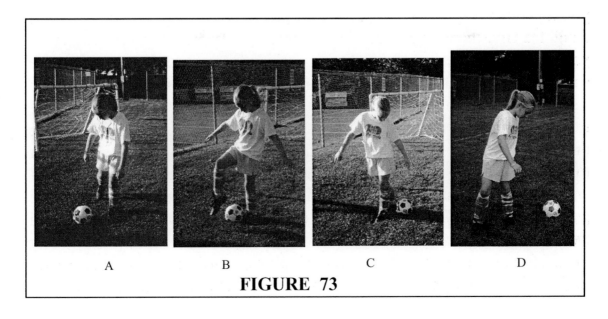

A   B   C   D

FIGURE 73

around the right side of the ball *(SEE FIGURE 73-B)*. When the right foot comes down, they balance and shift their weight to the left foot. Then they push the ball back behind them, and to their left, using the right foot *(SEE FIGURE 73-C)*. Next they pivot on the left foot, swing the right leg around, turn to their left, and start dribbling the ball to their left, using the outside of the left foot *(SEE FIGURE 73-D)*. They can switch, and dribble with the right foot, once they have made the turn, cleared the opponent, and have moved off to their left. When they have mastered this move with the right foot, you can try to reverse everything, and have them practice faking the kick with their left foot. Defenders, midfielders, backs, and all attacking players, should learn this technique.

A   B   C   D

FIGURE 74

Drills for Protecting the Ball

When you are on offense, and dribbling the ball up the field, you must protect the ball from being taken away (stolen) by an opposing player. The first rule is, keep your body between the ball and your opponent. This is because you are usually only guarded by one, opposing, player at a time. Turning sideways works best because that puts the most distance between you and your opponent. Don't stay in the same place too long. Anything over 5 seconds is too long. After that you need to move quickly to a new position where there is open space, and you have more room to pass the ball. If you see more than one

82

opposing player starting to close in to guard you, then you probably want to find one of your team mates, and loft a quick pass to them. It's very hard to protect the ball while dribbling when several opposing players are closing in on you.

Drill No. 55- Shielding the Ball

The Basics are:

This drill is just keeping the ball away from a defender, or opponent. Putting space between you and the opponent is what it's all about.

Practice:

To practice this technique, go out to a big back yard or a park area. And you, mom or dad, go to a spot about 3 or 4 yards behind, and to the right, of your son or daughter. Have them start dribbling the ball slowly forward, then you move up from behind them, and attempt to steal the ball away from them. When your son or daughter can see you coming up on them, out of the corner of their eyes, the should move over to the right side of the ball, and push it away from you using the outside of their left foot *(SEE FIGURE 74-A)*. Next they shield the ball from you by turning sideways, and spreading their feet to keep you away from the ball *(SEE FIGURE 74-B)*. After that they keep you away from the ball, with their right shoulder, while they start to turn and push the ball to their left *(SEE FIGURE 74-C)*. Then they pivot on the right foot, turn to their left, and dribble off to their left, starting with the outside of the left foot as they begin to dribble, to shield the ball from you *(SEE FIGURE 74-D)*. When they have mastered this move from the right side of the ball, you can try to reverse everything and have them practice protecting the ball from the left side. Defenders, midfielders, backs, and all attacking players, should learn this technique.

Drills for Running, Quickness and Endurance

When it comes down to it running, and endurance, is what soccer is all about. Players have to be in good shape, and have lots of stamina to keep up, especially in the later stages of the game. For soccer players, leg strength is more important than upper body strength. The whole game is mostly running, and the field is big. Speed is very important for all players, but especially for strikers and forwards. The following drills will improve on any players speed, quickness, and their basic running skills. Also remember to have them work on the coordination, agility, and field presence drills, along with the running drills because if they fall, or get tripped, it could save them from an injury. And these drills will help them to get right back up on their feet quickly, if they fall.

For most mom and dads, the back yard will not be long enough for these drills. Unless you have access to a regular, or a soccer practice, field that has white stripe yard marks, you will have to improvise. You will need to find a park or large grassy area, and estimate the necessary distances. Get molded plastic cleat high top soccer shoes if you can find them in small enough sizes, for your son or daughter to use *(SEE SECTION ON EQUIPMENT)*. Regular type tennis shoes tend to slip too much on grass, which will discourage them. The exception to this is, if they will be doing the running on artificial (Astro) turf, then running type or tennis shoes can work. One more point to make here, don't take them out to run in leather sole type street shoes. Sorry it won't do them, or the shoes, any good. They might even hurt themselves slipping with them on grass, and they could twist or sprain an ankles. Or they could even fall hard and hurt something else. However, even the tennis shoes will slip sometimes, and that is why we recommend the cleat type soccer shoes for grass.

Drill No. 56- Running Laps

The Basics are:

This drill of running laps is to keep their muscles warm and loose. It will also build their endurance, or stamina, up by doing lots of laps. However don't start them out with too many laps because you will wear them out, and then they may be discouraged on continuing this drill.

Practice:

A high school track is usually a quarter mile long for one lap around. We ran our 7 through 10 year old kids around a track of this size, at least two times, every night we practiced. I might point out here that these laps are to be run at a joggers pace and not at full speed. I think a 5 year old boy or girl should be able to do a least one lap a day on a quarter mile track, or an equivalent distance around a park or yard. When one lap is easy for them, then they can increase the distance, or number of laps. It is better to have them run laps around an oval shaped track, rather than a straight measured length. It will not seem as far to them as they go around, compared to a long straight measured length. Trust me it works better that way. This drill is even more important with heavier or over weight boys or girls. Its not how fast they go around, but making sure they go all the way around, without stopping, and at a comfortable speed. If your son or daughter gets discouraged, and you are able, you might try running with them for support. All players need to work on this drill.

Drill No. 57- Wind Sprints

The Basics are:
The wind sprint drill is a check on their speed. If you have access to a stopwatch, use it. If you don't have a stopwatch, then just use your wrist watch seconds hand, and check their time over a measured distance. For 5 and 6 year olds, I am going to recommend checking their speed over a 20 yard distance. For 7 and 8 year olds, I am recommending 30 yards. For 9

FIGURE 75

year olds and up, you could go up to 40 yards. You can use old one gallon white plastic milk cartons, filled with sand, "Kitty Litter", or water, and marked with the distance using a black wide tip permanent maker.

Practice:
To practice wind sprints find a large back yard, or a park. Then have your son or daughter get down into a runners start stance at the "0" yard marker *(SEE FIGURE 75).* Once you have a time, on them for these distances, make sure they use the same stance each time so the times will compare with each other. Stand at the end of the measured distance with your stopwatch, or wristwatch, and on the command "GO", have them fire out with an explode type move. Have them run as fast as they can until they pass you at the end distance yard marker. Do this as often as possible, so you can see if their speed is improving. All players need to work on this drill.

Drill No. 58- Wind Sprint Ladders

The Basics are:
This drill is called wind sprint ladders. If you don't have access to a field, with distance marked white yard line markers, this is going to be hard to set up. To do this you will need to buy, or make, your own "yard markers". Here is a suggestion if you will be doing this at a park, try using old white plastic milk bottles filled with sand, water, or "Kitty Litter", to weight it down. Then

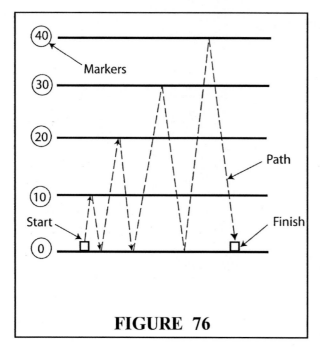

FIGURE 76

you can take a wide tip black felt permanent marker and mark 0, 10, 20, 30, 40, on them in big letters. They make great yard markers, and you are recycling for the environment. Next estimate a 40 yard distance. Put one bottle down at the starting point, then go down 40 yards and put another one down. Now in your mind, divide the distance between the two bottles into four equal spaces of 10 yards long. Then go out from the start 10 yards and put down a bottle, then go another 10 yards and put down another bottle, and so on. Now you have a 40 yard course set out. Here is how the ladders work.

Practice:

For practice have your son or daughter get at the starting point in a runners stance *(SEE FIGURE 75)*. On the command "GO" have them charge out straight ahead at full speed for 10 yards, then they stop quickly and touch either hand down on the ground. Then they turn around quickly and run back to the starting point. They will know when they have gone 10 yards, by looking over at the milk bottle. And the same look, over at the other markers, will let them know about where to touch down. Now, at the starting point, they stop again and quickly touch either hand down. Then they turn and run out to the 20 yard marker. Again they touch down, turn and run back to the starting point. Then they touch again, turn and run out to the 30 yard marker. Again they touch, turn and run back to the starting point. In other words they will be increasing the distance they run by 10 yards, each time they touch down at the starting point. The last time they will be running the whole 40 yards, then touching down and running 40 yards back to the starting point *(SEE FIGURE 76)*. Have them try to do a least one set of these every time you practice this drill. Later on if they can do more than one set and not be too tired, its ok. All players need to work on this drill.

Drill No. 59- Quickness Speed Bursts

The Basics are:

Quickness is really just speeding things up. These drills are designed to improve the quickness of all players. Speeding up drills already discussed, like Drill No. 56 ladders, will also improve on your son or daughters quickness. Generally speaking, any of the drills where they are exploding out of a stance, pivoting, spinning, twisting, or jumping can improve on their quickness when you keep speeding them up little by little. If they is not naturally quick, you will have to work hard with them to learn how to do this. However, keep being positive on reminding them that they are getting better, even if it is slowly. Be encouraging, by telling them they will learn, and to keep trying.

Here is one more quickness running drill. It is called speed bursts. It is really a lot like ladders. There are several variations, but I like this one best for young boys or girls. I have always ended up coaching the smaller kids, so that's why I am recommending this drill because I know it works. Start off by marking a 20 yard long course similar to the one discussed in drill No. 55, except put the yard markers at 5 yard intervals, instead of 10 yards apart.

Practice:

To practice this drill get the course marked first, then have your son or daughter get down into a runners stance at the "0" yard marker *(SEE FIGURE 75)*. On the command "GO", have them explode out from the starting marker and run, AS FAST AS THEY CAN for 5 yards, and pump their knees up high. Then have them stop and catch their breath while they turn and walk back to the 5 yards marker. Let them rest a minute or so, then say "READY", and have them quickly get down into their runners stance. As soon as he gets down say "GO", and have them run AS FAST AS THEY CAN back to the starting "0" yard marker. Then they stop again and walk slowly back to the starting "0" yard marker while catching their breath. Give them a minute or so to rest, then say "READY", followed with a "GO". They should explode out again, except this time they run out to the 10 yard marker and stop. Next they repeat the same burst back to the starting "0" yard marker. Keep them repeating these bursts, but increase the distance, by 5 yards down and back, each time until they get out to the 20 yard marker. Make sure they pump their hands up and down, and get their knees up as high as they can. One time all the way through the 20 yards, once a day, should be plenty to start with for most 5 year olds. All players need to work on this drill.

Drill No. 60- Endurance

The Basics are:

Endurance is really just how long you can go before you are too tired to go any farther. To build up their endurance, keep speeding up any of the drills little by little. If they get too tired doing any of the running, or quickness, drills, then stop the drill until they can build up their stamina, to get all the way through the drill one complete time. These drills will be tough on boys or girls that are big, and overweight, for their age. So be patient and keep encouraging them. Have them try going just a little bit farther, or faster, each day or week as you see that their stamina and endurance is building up.

Practice:

Drill No. 56 and 58 are especially good for building endurance. Or use any one of the drills you have been working with them on, speed them up a little, or increase the repetitions. All players need to work on this drill.

Drills for Chipping and Volleying

Chipping and volleying have to do with either kicking, or receiving, the ball in the air or on the ground. Or another way to look at it is, it's a different way of controlling balls in the air, or on the ground. The Chip kick is when contact is made when the ball is on the ground. The Volley kick is when contact is made when the ball is in the air. The reason I am putting these kicks in their own section is because are special technique kicks. They are used to make the ball do different things as compared to just kicking the ball. Remember when lofting the ball is mentioned, what we are talking about is chipping. As an example when you are dribbling the ball up field, then suddenly you see two players start to come over and challenge you or trap you, and you need to get the ball quickly over their heads to your team mate. What do you do. You quickly chip, or loft, the ball over their heads to the team mate that is in the clear. Chip kicks can also be used, to get the ball over a defensive wall of players in front of the goal, for a shot on goal.

A volley kick can also be used for a shot on goal because it's very quick, coming to you from in the air, and may catch a goalkeeper out of position. Or maybe you are way down near your own goal, and want to clear the ball out defensively. The volley can be used to make a long pass up the field.

Drill No. 61- Chipping the Ball

The Basics are:

This is the basic chip or loft kick. For a Chip kick you should come straight on to the ball, _not_ at an angle. Contact with the ball is when it is rolling on the ground. You can adjust the angle of the ball, or it's height, by how you lean. If you lean back, the ball takes a higher trajectory. If you lean forward, the ball takes a lower trajectory. This type of kick could be used to get the ball over a defender, or over a defensive wall, and in certain cases a short shot on goal.

A   **FIGURE 77**   B

Practice:

To practice this technique, go out to a big back yard or a park area, and you mom or dad, go to a spot about 8 or 10 yards out in front of your son or daughter. Take the ball and roll it very hard right at them. First thing to do is, have them get right _in front of_ the ball. Next have them come to the ball, and when they get close they plant the non-kicking left foot just to the side of the ball *(SEE FIGURE 77-A)*. Then have them bring the right kicking leg back, and use a shorter leg swing than they would normally use to kick the ball. Now, just as they start to make contact with the ball, they lean back and kick the underside of the ball using the instep part of the foot *(SEE FIGURE 77-B)*. All the way through the leg swing and follow through, they have to keep their eyes on the ball. The shorter the foot swing, and the farther they lean back, will determine the height and distance of the ball's trajectory. Have them try different foot swings, and leans, to get the feel of where the ball is going to go. If they use a very short leg swing, and hardly any follow through, the ball will go up much like a "Pop Fly" in baseball. When they have mastered kicking with the right foot, try to teach them to make the kick with the left foot. It will be harder to learn, but if they can, it will make them a better player. All players need to work on this drill.

Drill No. 62- Full Volley Kick
The Basics are:

This is the full volley kick. It means you kick the ball harder so it will go farther. This kick is similar to the "Hip Turn" kick. The difference is, you sort of stand more straight up and swivel the hips, rather than turning the whole body. Contact with the ball is while it is still in the air. As the ball is approaching, start to raise your kicking leg, with the knee going up first. As the ball meets the foot, you could twist the foot so that you contact the ball on the instep. This will let you kick the ball very solid, and hard, giving it lots of distance. Another technique is to contact the ball off the side of the foot, giving it a swiveling, spinning, action. This would tend to make the trajectory of the ball curve while in flight. This type of kick could be used for a pass, or a shot on goal.

Practice:

A   B   C

FIGURE 78

To practice this technique, go out to a big back yard or a park area, and you mom or dad, go to a spot about 10 or 20 yards out in front of your son or daughter. Take the ball and throw it to them so it comes in to them, in the air, about belt high. For a hard long distance straight right foot kick, have them get almost in front, but just a little to the left of where the ball will come down. Then they will tilt the body a little to their left *(SEE FIGURE 78-A)*, and raise the right leg knee first *(SEE FIGURE 77-A)*. Next they twist the hips, turn and square up to the ball, and aim at the ball so they make contact with the center instep part of their right foot *(SEE FIGURE 78-*

| STEP 1 | STEP 2 | STEP 3 |

FIGURE 79

B). For a long hard curving right foot kick, have them do everything the same as the straight kick, except meet the ball hard with the side of their foot *(SEE FIGURE 78-C)*. Have them keep working on these techniques until they can make them go straight, or curve while in flight. When they have mastered kicking with the right foot, then try to teach them to make the kicks with the left foot. It will be harder to learn, but if they can, it will make them a better player. Midfielders, and forwards, need to work on this drill.

Drill No. 63- Half Volley Kick
The Basics are:

This kick is just like the full volley, except contact is made on the first bounce. That is letting the ball almost get to you, except just after it hits and starts to bounce up, then you make contact. Depending on how you make the contact with the foot, the ball can go straight or curve. The technique is the same, except you let the ball hit the ground and catch it on the foot, just as it starts to come up on the first bounce.

Practice:

Practice this kick the same as the "full volley kick", except let the ball make the first bounce before you make the foot contact *(SEE FIGURE 79)*. This is kind of like the old football drop kick technique. When they have mastered kicking with the right foot, try to teach them to make the kicks with the left foot. It will be harder to learn, but if they can, it will make them a better player. Midfielders, and forwards, need to work on this drill.

Drills for Kicking & Shooting Goals

These drills are specifically for kicking and making shots on goal. This is what offensive soccer is all about, scoring points. It's kind of hard to win if you can't score any points. Basically there are two groups of kicks. First there are regular kicks on goal, then there are dead ball kicks. Regular kicks on goal are when a player is dribbling, or kicks, a moving ball down the field, right at the goal. Dead ball kicks are stationary kicks when the referee has given your team a free kick on a penalty. With regular kicks on goal there are a number of strategies and techniques. We will show each one separately. There are also different dead ball kick techniques. We will show them separately also.

Regular Kicks
Drill No. 64- Straight On or Angle Shots

The Basics are:

Straight on shots are where you dribble right up in front of the goal, or at an angle to the goal. These shots can be kicked with the instep of the foot *(SEE FIGURE 35)*, or the sides of the foot *(SEE FIGURES 36 & 37)*. Short kicks (up to 40 feet) are kicked hard, and usually aimed at either corner of the goal. This is because when the ball is aimed at the center of the goal, then the goalkeeper has a better chance of stopping it. Longer kicks (over 40 feet) should be kicked hard and aimed at the right, or the left half, of the goal. In particular, aim at the center of the space between the goalkeeper and the goal post. When you are about to make your kick, try to head and body fake the goalkeeper, by looking at the opposite corner from where you really want to aim before you start to swing the kicking foot. Also remember goalkeepers usually have a weak side, and most of the time that is their left side. So shoot towards your right hand side corner of the goal. Come up towards the goal dribbling. Do not stop to decide what you want to do. This just helps the defense.

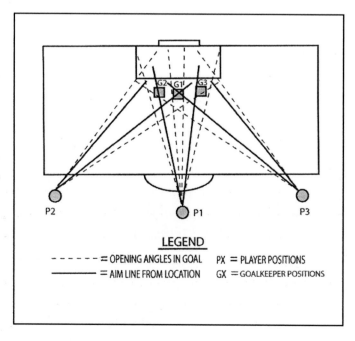

FIGURE 80

Decide, and figure out what you are going to do as you come up towards the goal.

Practice:

To practice this technique, first find a field with a full size goal on it (it is wider). Then have your son or daughter go out about 30 to 40 away, and practice the short kicks. Have them kick from right in front, on both sides, and at different angles *(SEE FIGURE 80)*. As an example when the player is at position "P1 ", and the goalkeeper is at position "G1", you would choose the aim lines to the right or to the left of "G1" *(SEE FIGURE 80)*. When the player is at position "P2", and the goalkeeper is at position "G2", you would choose the aim lines to the right or to the left of "G2" *(SEE FIGURE 80)*. Have them try kicking using the instep part of the foot *(SEE FIGURE 35)* and the inside part of the foot *(SEE FIGURE 36)*. This will let them know which technique works the best for them on the short kicks. The main thing they need to learn is where to aim the kick. It is a fact that around 80% of all goals are made in the 40 feet or under range. So focus your teaching on the short range kicks. Have them also get into the habit of faking just before they swing the foot. And especially make sure they learn how to make the kicks into the right corner of the goal (where it has the best chance of going in). This means they fake a kick into the left corner, then kick into the right corner. The exception is going to be if the goalkeepers strong side is his left side. Then you will have to aim for the left corner of the goal.

Next have them go out about 50 or 60 feet away and try the long kicks. On the longer kicks it is the instep part of the foot kick *(SEE FIGURE 35)* that has the most accuracy. The technique is the same as with the short kicks, except they just have to take better aim and kick harder because of the distance. Forwards, strikers, and wingbacks, need to work on this drill.

Drill No. 65- Off a Crossing Pass shot

The Basics are:

This is going to be much harder to learn than the rolling ball kicks. How it works is, first a team mate makes a crossing pass in the air. He aims or lofts the ball, to come down in the middle of the field, in front of the goal. The player, the pass is intended for, starts to run across the field towards where the pass will come down. This is a timing play. The player, and the pass in the air, must get arrive at the same time right in front of the goal. The player then has to make a quick decision whether to make the shot with the head, or the foot. See the

FIGURE 81

sections on *"Heading"* or on *"Chipping and Volleying"*, to see the techniques your son or daughter needs to use for making this shot.

Practice:

To practice this technique, first try to find a field with a full size goal on it (it is wider). Then have your son or daughter go out to a spot, on the left side of the goal, about 40 or 50 feet away if they are a right footed kicker *(SEE FIGURE 81)*. If they are a left footed kicker, have them go to the right side of the goal. This is because as you move towards the ball, you want to have the most kick technique options available to you on your strong foot side. Then you, mom or dad, stand across from them on the opposite side of the field so you are about 60 feet apart. Then have them start running towards you. Next lob the ball, in the air, to a point right in front of the goal. You will have to time your throw so that the ball gets there at the same time they do. Sometimes have them head the ball into the goal *(SEE FIGURE 49)*, then switch and have them kick it in *(SEE FIGURE 41 & 78)*. If they can't master this technique at first, keep working with them until they do. Forwards, strikers, and wingbacks, need to work on this drill.

Dead Ball Kicks

Drill No. 66- Direct Free Kicks
The Basics are:

The direct free kick is when only one player has to touch the ball on the kick. This is a free kick awarded when a penalty is called by the referee. Whether it is a direct or indirect free kick, will depend on how bad the rules violation was. To stop or block the direct free kick, the defense can put a wall of players right in front of the goal, at least 10 yards from the ball *(SEE FIGURE 82)*. The number of players in the wall, and exactly where it is placed, will depend on what the defensive tactic the coach wants to use. One technique for getting the ball around the player wall is, make a bending trajectory kick around the side of the player wall and into the corner of the goal. The other technique is, try to loft the ball over the heads of the players in the wall, and into the corner of the goal.

Practice:

To practice the bend around kick tech-

FIGURE 82

nique, first try to find a field with a full size goal on it (it is wider). You will then need at least 4 friends or helpers, about the same size as your son or daughter, to help out on this drill. First have your son or daughter take the ball, and go out to the penalty arc, or a spot about 60 or 70 feet right in front of the goal *(SEE FIGURE 82)*. Next have them set the ball down, then move back about 5 feet behind it and get ready to kick. The friends make a wall in front of the left side of the goal 10 yards from the ball *(SEE FIGURE 82)*. The other friend acts as the goalkeeper, and stands in back of the player wall. When they are ready, your son or daughter can make their kick. The technique for the bend around kick is to use the instep part of the foot. Contact is made to the center left or the center right on the ball. Hitting it on the left center, for a right foot kicker, should bend it more around to the right. And just the opposite for a right center contact kick. Your son or daughter is going to really have to focus on where they are contacting the ball, in order to make it curve or bend. If the player wall is over blocking the left corner of the goal, the kick should be aimed between the last man on the right

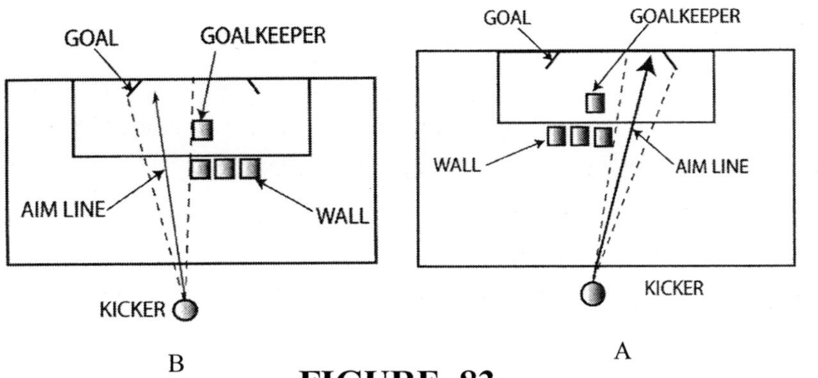

FIGURE 83

95

of the player wall and the right corner of the goal *(SEE FIGURE 83-A)*. If the player wall is over blocking the right corner of the goal, the kick should be aimed between the last man on the left of the player wall and the left corner of the goal *(SEE FIGURE 83-B)*. If they are having trouble learning to make this shot, keep working with them until they can master this technique.

To practice the loft over the top kick, set the wall of players, and goal-keeper, up just like for the bend around kick. The difference is going to be the technique used for the kick. For this technique use a chip kick *(SEE FIGURE 77)*. They will have to practice this kick many times, to get the ball to go over the heads, and the body, of the players in the wall. If they are having trouble learning to make this shot, keep working with them until they can master this technique. All players except goalkeepers, and sweepers, need to work on both of these shot techniques.

Drill No. 67- Indirect Free Kick

The Basics are:

The indirect free kick is when at least one other player, from either team, has to touch the ball after the kicker has made the first kick. The second or third player must touch the ball before it goes into the goal in order that the goal counts *(SEE FIGURE 84)*. This is a free kick awarded when a penalty is called by the referee. Whether it is a direct or indirect free kick will depend on how bad the rules violation was. To stop or block the indirect free kick, the defense can put a wall of players no closer than 10 yards from the ball until it is in play, unless they are in front of the goal between the posts *(SEE FIGURE 84)*. See the direct free kick section for the different types of kicks used to score on this type of dead ball kick. The only real difference between the two kicks is the second, or third, touching of the ball on the indirect free kick. The kick technique, used by whoever makes the kick into the goal, is the same.

Practice:

To practice the indirect free kick you (mom or dad) will need at least 4 friends, and ideally 6

FIGURE 84

96

friends to help out. The friends should be the same size as your son or daughter. First have your son or daughter take the ball, and go out to the penalty arc, or a spot about 60 or 70 feet right in front of the goal *(SEE FIGURE 84)*. Next have them set the ball down, then move back about 5 feet behind it, and get ready to kick. Have at least three of, the friends make a wall in front of the left side of the goal *(SEE*

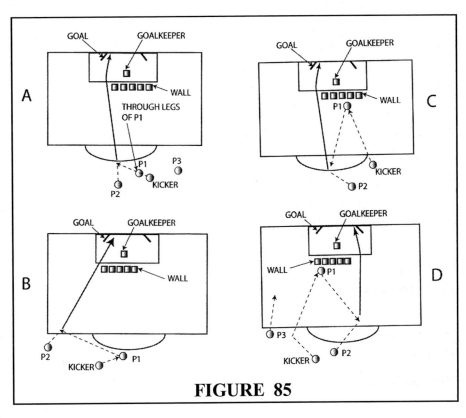

FIGURE 85

FIGURE 84). The other friend can act as the goalkeeper, and stand in back of the player wall. If you can't find the 6 friends to help out, get at least 2 friends, then work just on setting up the passing plays for the shot on goal. Here is four passing plays, you can use to set up the kick into the goal *(SEE FIGURE 85)*. The first play *(FIGURE 85-A)* is where the kicker kicks the ball between the legs of a faking P1 moving to the left, through to a spot where P2 comes up and bends a kick around the wall into the left corner of the goal. The second play *(FIGURE 85-B)* is where the kicker fakes going to the right, then passes to P1, who passes over to a spot where P2 comes up, and kicks into the left corner of the goal. The third play *(FIGURE 85-C)* is where the kicker fakes a shot, passes to P1, who passes back to P2, who comes up and bends a kick around the wall, and into the left corner of the goal. The fourth play *(FIGURE 85-D)* is where the kicker fakes going to the left, passes to P1, who passes to a spot where P2 comes up, then bends a kick around the wall and into the right corner of the goal. P3 fakes going for a kick into the left corner of the goal, to fake the goalkeeper out of position. All players except goalkeepers, and sweepers, need to practice these techniques.

Drill No. 68- Corner Kick

The Basics are:

A corner kick is awarded to the offensive team when a defensive player kicks, or last touches, the ball when it goes across the field end line. The ball is then placed, on the ground, in the corner circle nearest where the ball left the field of play. The player, making the kick, should place the ball where the corner flag does not obstruct their approach to the kick. There is ideal ball placement locations for right, and left, footed kickers *(SEE FIGURE 86)* within the corner circle. It is legal though to place a ball right on the field or corner circle lines. However there is not much advantage for young kids to do this. There is many tactics and techniques used for corner kicks. We will show four of the more common plays you can use for corner kicks *(SEE FIGURE 87)*.

The first play *(SEE FIGURE 87-A)* is where the kicker (K) kicks a bending curving kick to a spot near the front of the goal, then either P1, P2, or P3, goes to the ball and heads it in, or kicks it in. The

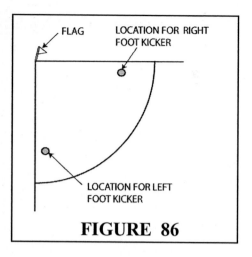

FIGURE 86

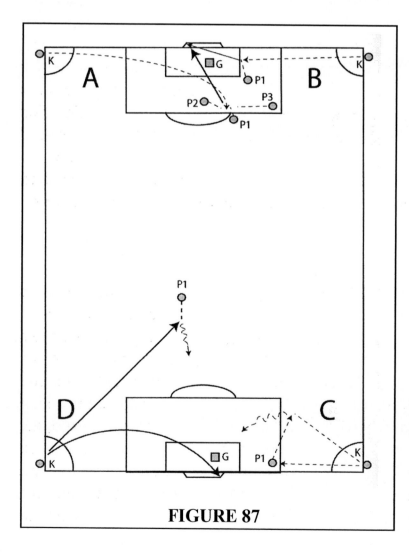

FIGURE 87

second play *(SEE FIGURE 87-B)* is where the kicker (K) places a head high pass right at the goalkeeper, then P1 comes up and either backwards heads, or kicks, the ball into the goal. The third play *(SEE FIGURE 87-C)* is where the kicker (K) passes to P1, who passes back to the kicker (K) who has moved towards the corner of the penalty area, who then dribbles toward the goal for a pass to a team mate, or a shot on goal. The fourth play *(SEE FIGURE 87-D)* is where the kicker (K) either

FIGURE 88

makes a long curving bending kick directly into the goal, or makes a safe pass back to an midfielder P1, who then passes off to a forward, or striker, who sets up a play for a kick on goal. There are several things to point out here, to make the long direct kick into the goal, the kicker makes contact on the ball with the lower instep part of the foot, and just below the center of the ball *(SEE FIGURE 88)*. This should be just about where the shoe laces begin. The kicker also needs to lean back a bit, to get height to the trajectory of the ball. The kicker should see where the defense is lined up before he makes the kick. This is because a defensive player can get as close as 10 yards from the ball before it is kicked. They do this to obstruct the kickers view, and to block the kick if they can.

FIGURE 89

Practice:

To practice the corner kicks, first explain to your son or daughter what all the kicker and team player options are. To do this, go over the diagram in *FIGURE 87*. Probably the first play to practice is the long bending, curving, kick into the goal. Find a full size goal to kick into if you can. Otherwise use a smaller practice goal. Place a cone out about 15 yards right in front of the goal. Then line it up on a line to the center of the goal. Next have your son or daughter stand about 15 yards behind the cone, and in line with the center of the goal. Set the ball down on the ground about 5 feet in front of them. Now they are ready to take the kick. If they are a right footed kicker, they take a side step to their left. Left footed kickers just the opposite. What they are trying to do is, kick the ball slightly to the right of the cone, then have it curve around the cone to the left and into the goal *(SEE FIGURE 89)*. The cone is just an object to gage if the kick is curving in it's flight towards the goal. Check on the diagram in *FIGURE 87,* on where to aim the leg swing. Right footed kickers should make the hit on the ball to the outside (right) center area. Left footed kickers just the opposite. For the real little kids, I suspect it will take a lot of trial and error practice to learn this technique. However if you start working with them at 5 years old, they might be pretty good at it by the time they get to their first team. Another learning technique is to have them walk up in slow motion, then stop, and show them how their foot has to be bent back. Then where to make the correct hit contact with the ball. After they have practiced the kick technique awhile, have them get 2 or 3 of their friends about their same size, then practice the four plays in *FIGURE 87*. All players except goalkeepers, and sweepers, need to practice these techniques.

Drill No. 69- Penalty Kick

The Basics are:

A penalty kick is awarded when a defensive player fouls the offensive player while in their own penalty area of the field. It is usually a direct free kick for the offensive team. The difference is the kicker (K) and the goalkeeper (G) are the only ones allowed in the penalty area. If the kicker is clever, it gives them an excellent chance for a goal. The penalty kicks are almost always direct free kicks. However, there can be an indirect free kick, but is very seldom ever awarded. The most often used technique for the kicker is, to aim the shot at either corner of the goal. Since most goalkeepers have a weak side to their left because they are right handed, it's a good idea to look fake the kick towards the left corner of the goal. Then take the shot into the right corner. During the penalty kick the offside rule is in effect. What this means is, no offensive player can be closer to the goal than the last defensive player. This gives both the offensive, and defensive, players an equal chance at handling a ball bouncing off the goal post. Or a ball knocked away by the goalkeeper. For a typical alignment for a penalty kick *SEE FIGURE 90.*

Practice:

To practice penalty kicks see the section for practicing the direct free kick *(PAGE 95)*. The only difference is, you don't have to practice bending a kick around a wall of players. You just need a helper playing goalkeeper, standing right in the middle of the goal. Make sure you practice this play in a full sized goal though because you will need

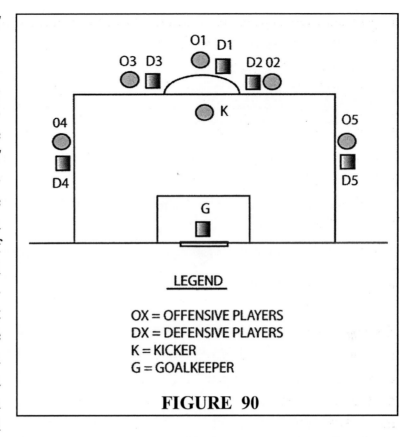

FIGURE 90

the extra room to try to kick it into the corners. All players except goalkeepers, and sweepers, need to practice this techniques.

Drills for Goalkeeping

Goalkeeping is a very important part of the game of soccer. A great goalkeeper can win the game for a team. It is a specialized position. The goalkeeper has to be a very good athlete. He is the last person on defense, to keep the opposing team from scoring. When young kids are just starting out, usually the best athlete on the team ends up being the goalkeeper. This is because they need a wide variety of skills. They have to be quick, and very focused. They have to be able to kick the ball, catch the ball, and block shots on goal. They are the only person on the team, except for the "throw in" person that is allowed to use their hands. Since most of the techniques used by goal keepers have to do with "catching", and "receiving", lets start with them first.

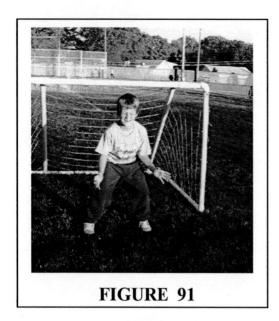

FIGURE 91

Catching

Drill No. 70- Ready Position
The Basics are:

The ready position lets the goalkeeper get ready to catch the ball, and move in any direction. The feet should be about shoulder width apart, with the knees slightly bent. You should be balanced with your weight shifted slightly forward, and up on the balls of your feet. This is so you can quickly push off in any direction *(SEE FIGURE 91)*. Your arms should be slightly bent, and out at your sides. When assuming this position try to be alert, but relaxed. If you are stiff and tight you will have problems. The hands should be in the open position, with the palms facing the oncoming ball or shooter. However, avoid trying to catch a ball, with the thumbs pointing straight towards the direction the ball is coming from. Always shift your arms so that the thumbs are pointed up. The eyes should be basically straight ahead, but focused on either the incoming ball or player.

Practice:

To practice this technique, have your son or daughter stand in front of you several yards. Next say "ready", then have them quickly get in this position. Check and make sure their feet, hands, eyes, and palms, are correctly positioned. Goalkeepers, and sweepers, need to work on this drill.

Drill No. 71- Belt and Chest High Catches
The Basics are:

On incoming balls right at you around belt and chest high, catch the ball by letting it come into your midsection. Then curl both hands and arms underneath, up, and then around it *(SEE FIGURE 92),*

FIGURE 92

102

cradling it to your body. However, catch it like you would an egg that you did not want to break. You do this by absorbing the force, and cushioning the balls impact. This is called a soft handed catch. If you try to catch the ball with stiff hands and arms, it might bounce off and back to the kicker, and giving them another chance at scoring. Look the ball all the way into your hands. If you take your eyes off the ball before you have secured it, to see where opposing players are, there is a chance of it bouncing off your hands or chest.

Practice:

To practice this technique, have your son or daughter stand out in front of you about 15 to 20 yards. Say "Ready", then have them quickly get into the position. Next, mom or dad, throw the ball at them at chest height. Make sure they are first looking the ball all the way into their chest area. Then make sure they curl their hands up, and around the ball, correctly. Remember though this is only on balls that come almost directly at them. If the ball goes way out to the side of them, or over their head, they need to use one of the other techniques of catching the ball. Also check and make sure they are soft catching the ball as they bring it in. Just goalkeepers need to work on this technique.

Drill No. 72- Low Catches

The Basics are:

On incoming balls that are below the waist, slightly to one side or the other, or rolling on the ground, catch the ball by first going sideways to get in front of it. Then go down on one knee *(SEE FIGURE 93-A)*. Next bring both hands down under the ball , then curl them up to your chest after you have secured it *(SEE FIGURE 93-B)*. Look the ball all the way into your hands. If you take your eyes off the ball before you have secured it, to see where opposing players are, there is a chance of it

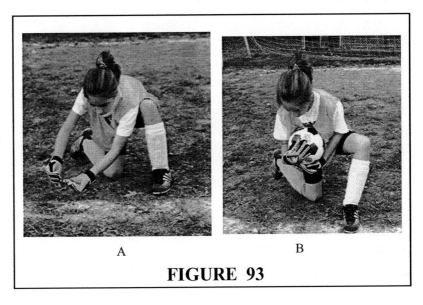

A B

FIGURE 93

bouncing off your hands, or chest, then back out to the opposing team.

Practice:

    To practice this technique, have your son or daughter stand out in front of you about 15 to 20 yards. Say "Ready", then have them quickly get into the position *(SEE FIGURE 91)*. Then throw the ball slightly to one side or the other of them. Make it low, or rolling on the ground. Make sure they first go sideways to get in front of the ball. Next make sure they go down on one knee, and look the ball into their hands. After that make sure they get both hands down under the ball, then curl the hands back up to their chest when they have secured it. Just goalkeepers need to work on this technique.

Drill No. 73- Over the Head Catches

The Basics are:

    On incoming balls way over your head, you will need to jump way up to catch it. First thing you need to do is go sideways, if you need to, in order to get in front of the ball. Next they have to jump way up high to catch it.

Practice:

    To practice this technique, have your son or daughter stand out in front of you about 15 to 20 yards. Say "Ready", then have them quickly get into the position *(SEE FIGURE 91). Then* throw the ball first right over the top of their head, then next slightly to one side or the other of them. On the balls right over the top of their head, they jump straight up in the air leading with their strong side leg first *(SEE FIGURE 94-A)*. For right handed player, the right leg (most). For left handed players the left leg. Once they get up into the air, they reach way up as far as necessary with both hands to catch the ball *(SEE FIGURE 94-B)*. On balls slightly to one side or the other of

B   A

FIGURE 94

them, they need to first go sideways to get in front of the ball. Then they jump up off of one leg first.

If the ball goes to their right, they jump with the right leg up first. If the ball goes to their left, they jump up with the left leg first. By doing this they get the best push of in that direction. Last they bring both hands up, leading with the hand on the same side as the up leg. This is going to take some time to teach the real young kids because they will usually want to raise up their strong side leg first, no matter which side the ball goes on. This is like teaching baseball players to be switch hitters. This means their weak side will not be so weak. Being a switch jumper gives them a slight advantage over a regular goalkeeper. Just goalkeepers need to work on this technique.

Drill No. 74- Diving Catches

The Basics are:

On incoming balls way off to either side of you, a diving way out sideways move will be needed. From the ready position *(SEE FIGURE 91)* you have to be on the balls of your feet, in order to push off very quickly to either side. These catches are sometimes referred to as "three handed Catches". This is because you trap the ball against the ground, which becomes the third hand.

Practice:

To practice this technique, have your son or daughter stand out in front of you about 15 to 20 yards. Say "Ready", then have them quickly get into the position *(SEE FIGURE 91).* ***Then*** throw a ground ball first to their right, then to their left. Throw it just far enough to the side of them that they have to dive to catch the ball *(SEE FIGURE 95)*. Their first move is to step out with the foot on the side where the ball is. If they can reach the ball, they push off right away with the lead foot and dive as far out as they can *(SEE FIGURE 95-A)*. Next they extend both hands out as far as they can, palms open, to reach and catch the ball *(SEE FIGURE 95-B)*. If it appears the ball is going to be farther away than a step, dive, and reach, then

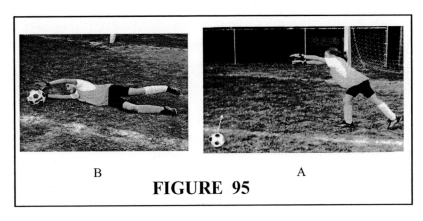

B   A
FIGURE 95

A   B

FIGURE 96

they may have to take a few cross over steps, to gain speed, then dive for the ball. The only way they will learn how to judge a dive for a ball is, having someone work many many times with them, on balls way off to their sides. Since the majority of kids are right handed, work the hardest on their weak side, which is to their left. Lots of shots on goal are rolling on the ground balls, way away from them into the corner of the goal. So they really need to work hard on this technique in order to be effective in stopping the shot. Just goalkeepers need to work on this technique.

Here is a very good drill your son or daughter can work on all by themselves, to practice catching balls. How they do this is, have them sit down on the ground, with both legs spread way apart. Then take the ball in both hands and bounce it down on the ground right between their legs *(SEE FIGURE 96-A)*. They need to bounce it as hard as they can so that it goes way up in the air. As soon as they bounce it, they get up as fast as they can, jump up, and try to catch the ball at it's highest point in the air. Both hands should be extended when they catch it *(SEE FIGURE 96-B)*.

Deflecting Shots

Deflecting shots is another technique the goalkeeper has to stop the opposing team from scoring. The two most common ways to do this is, using the fist or the palm of the hand. Remember though you only want to deflect balls that are coming in too high, or too hard, to catch. The high ball is deflected over the cross bar and top of the goal net. Medium height, and low, balls are deflected around to the sides of the goal. This is a very dangerous deflection though because it might accidentally go right to an opposing player for another shot on goal. The goalkeeper has to know where their close by team mates are at all times while they are being attacked. So they can deflect the ball right to the team mate if necessary. Another not to often used deflection is, blocking and deflecting a ball, off the foot of an opposing player dribbling the ball into the penalty zone for a shot on goal. You would probably only need to use this technique if you get caught too far out away from the goal.

Drill No. 75- Punching the Ball
The Basics are:

One of the techniques for stopping shots on goal is, punching the ball away. You might use this technique when it looks like you might not be able to reach, and catch the ball, with both hands. You do this by making a fist, then punching at the ball with the hand nearest to it *(SEE FIGURE 97)*. The punch should be aimed at where you want it to go. Contact should be right in the center of the ball, if possible because this way it will tend to go right where it is aimed.

FIGURE 97

Practice:

To practice this technique, have your son or daughter stand out in front of the goal. Then you, Mom or dad, go out to a spot about 15 to 20 yards in front of them. Say "Ready", then have them quickly get into the ready position *(SEE FIGURE 91)*. Then throw the ball to them, at about knee to head height. First throw it slightly to their right side, then to their left side. When the ball is to their right side have them make a fist, then punch the ball just around the right side of the goal. When the ball goes to their left side they should punch the ball

A   B

FIGURE 98

107

FIGURE 99

away, using their left fist. Make sure they understand that they have to make contact right in the center of the ball while aiming it at spot where they want it to go. And their follow through, with the arm and fist, should be pointed right in the direction you want the ball to go in. Just goalkeepers need to work on this technique.

Drill No. 76- Deflecting with the Palm

The Basics are:

Deflecting the ball with the palm, or palms of the hand, is mostly used for hard high balls that you might not be able to reach with both hands. Rather than having the ball go over your hands into the top part of the goal, you deflect it up, out, and over the top of the goal. You do this by using the open palm of your hand. When the ball comes in way up high, hard, and right at you, use two hands. Make the contact with the palms up, the fingers out, and underneath the ball *(SEE FIGURE 98-A)*. Then you just lift the ball up, over, and behind you volley ball style *(SEE FIGURE 98-B)*. If the ball comes in and you have to lunge or dive for it, then use just one hand and palm *(SEE FIGURE 99)*. When softer lob shots come in, or shots drifting down into the goal, then turn sideways and use one hand to lift it over the crossbar *(SEE FIGURE 100)*.

Practice:

To practice this technique find a full sized goal, then have your son or daughter stand out in front. Then you, Mom or dad, go out to a spot about 10 yards in front of them. Say "Ready", then have them quickly get into the ready position *(SEE FIGURE 91)*. Then throw the ball to them, first very hard throws right over the top of their head. As soon as they see it's going way over their head, have them rotate the hands, fingers down, palms in, and thumbs out *(SEE FIGURE 98-A)*. Then just as the ball gets to them, they jump

FIGURE 100

up, bring both hands underneath the ball, and lift it up over the top of the crossbar *(SEE FIGURE 98-B)*.

After they have they have tried the volleyball type deflection a few times, then throw the ball at them, first to the right then the left. Throw it at about waist to shoulder height. What you want them to do is dive for the ball, then extend one arm and palm out to deflect it *(SEE FIGURE 99),* using the arm and palm on the side the ball is on. Where they want to deflect it is just to the outside of the goal. Have them try the right side, then the left side.

To practice the soft lob deflection, you will have to maybe get a little closer, then underhand lob the ball right at them. And make sure it is just over their head because they are practicing deflecting, and not catching, on this drill. Just when it comes in, they want to first turn sideways. Then using the open hand, and palm, deflect it right over the crossbar *(SEE FIGURE 100)*. On this technique, what they need to learn how to do is, become a "switch" deflector. Once they learn how to do this with lots of practice, it will become a habit. I admit though there will be some kids that just will not be able to master the switching part of the technique. Here is what they need to learn. When the ball comes in, slightly to their left side, they turn to the left and push the ball over with the right hand. Now here comes the hard part for right handed players's. When the ball comes in, slightly to their right side, they turn to the right and push the ball over with the left hand. Young kids can learn how to do this if you keep working with them over and over. If they are having trouble learning this, you might want to stand up very close to them, and try this in a slow motion. Walk them through it until they get the feel of how to make the moves. Just goalkeepers need to work on this technique.

Distributing the Ball

When the goalkeeper makes a clean save (they do not drop the ball),

STEP 1 STEP 2

FIGURE 101

STEP 1   STEP 2

FIGURE 102

they want to quickly get the ball back out and upfield. They have 6 seconds to get the ball out of the penalty area. If they are clever in doing this, then they can catch the opposing team off guard.

Drill No. 77- Distributing

The Basics are:

Distributing the ball is just getting it out to their team mates. To do this they can throw the ball , or roll it, to a team mate, or kick the ball out and way up field. To see the different techniques for throwing the ball *SEE DRILLS IN THE SECTION FOR THROWING.* They can also kick the ball out to either a team mate up field, or to a clear space up field. When they kick the ball it can be placed on the ground and kicked *(SEE FIGURE 101)* or it can be drop kicked. The drop kick is where you drop, or bounce, the ball on the ground. As it bounces up you kick it *(SEE FIGURE 102)*.

Practice:

To practice these techniques, have your son or daughter take the ball and go to a spot right in front of the goal, within the box. Next you, mom or dad, go out to a spot about 15 yards in front of them. Then have them first practice rolling the ball out to you. Next have them side arm throw the ball out to you *(SEE FIGURE 55)*. After that have them throw the ball out to you with a two handed overhead throw *(SEE FIGURE 54)*. Then next have them make a one hand overhand throw to you *(SEE FIGURE 56)*. Last have them place the ball on the ground, and practice kicking the ball *(SEE FIGURE 101)*. To get more lift for a long kick, contact has to be on the lower half of the ball. Have them lean back just as they make the long kick, which helps to make the ball go up higher in the air. Also move around to different spots and make sure they can get the kick right to you. And just to make sure they know all the basics, have them practice a drop kick out to you *(SEE FIGURE 102)*. To make this kick, you can just lean slightly over, drop the ball using both hands, then when it bounces up you time your foot swing to meet the ball about 4 to 6 inches off the ground. This may be real hard for the little kids to learn. So, if they are 5, 6, or 7, and can't master this technique, don't worry about it. Just make sure they understand that this is a legal technique to use for a distribution kick. Just goalkeepers need to work on all these techniques.

Goal Kicks

When an opposing player kicks the ball out of bounds over the end line next to your goal, you get a free kick. This is called a goal kick. The goalkeeper usually makes this kick. This is really just a clearance kick, to get the ball way out away from your goal.

Drill No. 78- Goal Kick

The Basics are:

They place the ball on the ground, within the goal box *(SEE FIGURE 101)*. The placement is usually right up on the front line of the goal box. To get lots of power for a long kick, make sure they have a good hard follow through with the kicking foot. They should be looking for a team mate way down the field, or just kick the ball straight ahead as far down the field as they can.

Practice:

Practice this kick with them the same way you would, with the placed on the ground distribution kick, as explained *IN DRILL NO. 77.*

Goalkeeper Defensive Techniques

In this section we will cover some of the basic defensive techniques and tactics a goalkeeper needs to know. How they position themselves in the box, and also in front of the goal is very important. They should know this for penalty kicks and shots on goal. There are tactics for stopping dribbling forwards coming in to make a shot on goal. They should know the basic tactics for offensive play in front of the goal. They should know how to position team mates for a "wall" against free kicks.

Drill No. 79- Position Around the Goal

The Basics are:

The goalkeeper must know the right position to be in around the goal so that the advantage goes to them, rather than the shooter. To determine where they should be, imagine a line from the center of the goal out to the middle of the penalty box front line. Now you have a right half zone and a left half zone *(SEE FIGURE 103)*. Here are some basic or general rules a goalkeeper can follow:

- *When the ball is in the opposing teams half of the field, the goal keeper comes up to the line on the front part of the goal box area. This is especially important when their team is not using a sweeper. This is so they can catch any long loose passes.*

- *When the ball is in your half of the field up to about 30 yards in front of the goal, the goalkeeper remains up in the front part of the goal box.*

- *When the opponent is moving with the ball, and gets to the penalty area, the goalkeeper runs right at him in way to cut down the angle of a shot on goal (SEE FIGURE 103). The problem with this technique is, if the goalkeeper's timing is not just right, the approaching player with the ball can loft a kick over the goalkeeper's head and into the goal.*

Another way the goalkeeper can position themselves is, to stand back in the center of the goal at "G1" *(SEE FIGURE 103)*. Then if the shooter comes into the left zone at "P3", the goalkeeper moves to position "G3" to cut down the angle of the shot *(SEE FIGURE 103)*. And if the shooter "P2" comes into the right zone area, the goalkeeper moves to "G2" position to cut down the on that angle of the kick *(SEE FIGURE 103)*.

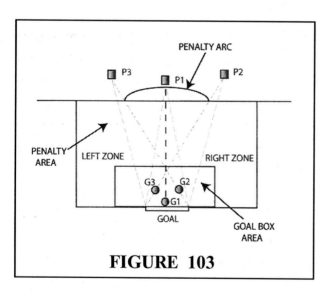

FIGURE 103

The position of a goalkeeper's own defensive players will tell them where to be positioned. Here are some basic rules for the goalkeeper to follow, by observing where the nearby players on their team are located:

- *As long as one of the goalkeeper's team mates are marking (Covering) the opponent with the ball, the goalkeeper can stay in the front center area of the goal box.*

- *If one of the goalkeeper's team mates is covering part of the goal, say the left zone side, the goalkeeper can move over to the "G2" area to cover the other side of the goal. And just the reverse for covering the left side in the "G3" area (SEE FIGURE 103). This applies when they are sure a team mate is covering the other zone side*

Practice:

To practice these rules you (mom or dad) could set up a system of "Call outs". You may need a helper, to move around the different positions while you observe. How this would work is, have your son or daughter go stand right in center of the goal (G1). Then you would say **"Their half"**, and they would move to the front line of the goal box. Then you could say **"Our half"**, and they stay right where they are. Or you say **"Box"**, and they would run right at a helper, acting as a shooter, and block or tackle the ball. After you make the call, see if they go to the right place on the field. Just goalkeepers need to work on all these techniques.

Drill No. 80- Stopping Penalty Kicks

The Basics are:

For penalty kicks, the position of the kicker will tell the goalkeeper where to position themselves. Where the kicker is on the penalty arc dictates their position. If the kicker is in the center area of the penalty arc (P1), then the goalkeeper can stay right in front of the goal at position "G1" *(SEE FIGURE 103)*. If the kicker is in the left zone area side of the penalty arc, then the goal-keeper takes the position "G3" . If the kicker is in the right zone area of the penalty arc, the goalkeeper goes to position "G2".

Practice:

Practice for this technique the same way you would practice "catching", and deflecting, techniques in *DRILL 70-76*. Except you (mom or dad), or whoever makes the kick at them needs to place the ball at different spots around the penalty arc. This gives them practice with kicks coming from all directions. Just goalkeepers need to

FIGURE 104

work on all these techniques.

Drill No. 81- Stopping Dribbling Forwards

The Basics are:

There is several ways of stopping a dribbling forward, or shooter. The obvious, of course, is to stand right in the center of the goal and wait for them to make their shot. The other way is to run directly right at them when they get in to the penalty box area. Then when they get close enough to the dribbling player, they block the ball and catch it if they can *(SEE FIGURE 104)*.

Practice:

To practice this technique, have your son or daughter go to the front of the goal box. Next you, mom or dad, go out to the front of the penalty box and start dribbling the ball right at the goal. Don't take the shot though because they need to practice their blocking technique. What they want to do, depending on which side or foot you are dribbling with, is wait until you get about a yard away, then drop down and smother or block the ball. If you are dribbling with the right foot, as most player are, they dive down to their left and spread their hands out with open palms *(SEE FIGURE 104)*. Notice how the hands are positioned to protect the goalkeeper's face. Tell them when they get close, within a few yards away from you, to watch only the ball and not your eyes. By focusing on the ball, their hands will go right to the ball. And they won't be faked out of position, and miss the ball. As they hit the ground, they use the left arm to cushion the fall, and block the ball from getting out to the their left *(SEE FIGURE 104)*. After they practice diving to their left, then switch off and dribble at them with your left foot. They would then dive to their right to block the ball. Make sure they are blocking and recovering the ball because if they miss, it's a clear shot at the goal for the shooter. This is why it is so important to just watch the ball when they get close.

Drill No. 82- Building a Wall

The Basics are:

The defensive wall we discussed in the section on "dead ball kicks" found in *Drill No. 66*, has it's own rules and techniques. That is what we will go over in this section. The goalkeeper is like the quarterback of the defense. So they should be the player to direct where they want the wall. I know this is going be hard for little kids learn, especially at 5 or 6 years old. However, they have to start sometime to learn the strategies and tactics of goalkeeping. With your help, mom or dad, they can learn the basics. The wall is a technique to stop a free kick. The way the goalkeeper would position the wall is, they call out the name of one of the END players on the wall. They would say, "Joey move to the left or to the right", meaning the whole wall would then move with Joey, in whichever direction he moves *(SEE FIGURE 105)*. The other strategy is to have a team mate standing behind the penalty kicker

FIGURE 105

give direction on where to move the wall. The thinking here seems to be, that a player standing behind the kicker is in a better position than the goalkeeper, to position where the wall needs to be placed.

Then there are strategies within the wall players, as a group. Usually the tallest players are placed on the edges or corners of the wall *(SEE FIGURE 106)*. The players in the wall can not jump up and block a kick, using their hands. In fact if it looks like they have used their hands, in any way to block or deflect the ball, a penalty may be called. So what many players do is, grasp their hands together and lower them all the way down *(SEE FIGURE 106)*. Or they may stiffen their arms and keep them at their sides *(SEE FIGURE 107)*. Players in the wall have to be very tough. If they even raise their hands in front of their face to protect it, and the ball is deflected off of their hands, a penalty usually is called. So they have to just let the ball hit them. They can jump way up high in the air to block or deflect a kick *(SEE FIGURE 107)*. When the kick is from the penalty arc area, some teams use 7 or 8 players in

FIGURE 106

FIGURE 107

the wall to get the most protection. When the kick is coming from between the penalty box and a sideline, use at least 3 players in the wall.

Practice:

It may be hard to get 5 or 6 of your son or daughters friends to come over to practice this technique. If that is the case, then set them down, and go over what is expected from them when they are one of the players in the wall. Otherwise practice them in grasping, and putting, their hands together. Then go out to about where the front edge of the goal box would be, and throw a ball at them, then make sure they keep their hands away from the ball. Also make sure they learn to jump way up high to block or deflect the ball. It might also be a good idea to have them get in a line, with 4 or 5 of their friends, then call them out by name and say, "Jimmy move to your right". Your son or daughter, along with their friends, then move to their right. Or you could call out your son or daughter by name, then with arm directions, signal them which direction you want them to move in. All players, including the goalkeeper, need to practice this technique. This would especially include kids that are tall for their age.

Drills for the Kickoff

There is a kickoff at the start of every game, and the restart after halftime. There is also a kickoff after each period, or when a goal is scored. What we will talk about here is some of the basic techniques, and tactics, young players need to know and practice.

Drill No. 83- Offensive Techniques and Tactics

The Basics are:

First thing to remember is, you have to be on your side of the field halfway line. Next remember the player making the kick has to kick it forward. Once the kicker has kicked the ball, they can not touch it again until at least one defensive or offensive player has touched it. What usually happens in youth soccer is, the kicker kicks the ball slightly forward, but sideways, right in front of a team mate next to them (P1). Then that player kicks the ball back to the kicker *(SEE FIGURE 108-A)*. This seems to be because the best scoring player on the team usually is the kicker in youth soccer. And the coach wants one of their best scorers to handle the ball as much as possible. The kicker then dribbles down the field and looks for a play to make.

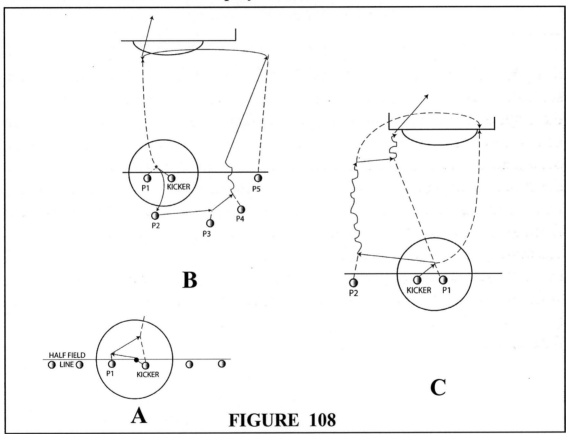

FIGURE 108

Another play right off the kickoff is, the kicker kicks the ball slightly forward but sideways, right in front of a team mate next to them (P1). The kicker then continues on down the field towards the left side of the goal. P1 passes the ball back to P2, who passes the ball over to P3, who passes over to P4, who dribbles the ball for a short distance. P4 then makes a curving kick to P5, who has moved way down to the right side of the field, who then passes over to the kicker ,who has moved way down the field to the left side of the penalty arc. The kicker then takes a shot on goal *(SEE FIGURE 108-B)*.

This play right off the kickoff is designed to confuse the defense by miss-direction, then spread them out all over the field. The kicker kicks the ball slightly forward but sideways, right in front of their team mate (P1) next to them. P1 then kicks the ball over to P2, who has moved down the field a short distance. P2 then dribbles the ball downfield towards the left flank side of the goal. P2 then passes the ball over across field to the P1, who has moved down to the front left side of the penalty arc. Then P2 continues on through the penalty area, and around towards the right side of the penalty box. The kicker has moved to this area also, then this pulls a lot of player with them over to the right side of the field, thinking that is where the play is going. P1 then dribbles right to the edge of the penalty box, and takes a shot on goal *(SEE FIGURE 108-C)*.

Practice:

You can practice these plays if you have access to a soccer field with a goal, and with a lot of your son or daughters friends to act as helpers. However, since this is not usually possible most of the time, you will probably just have to sit down with them, and go over the diagrams. If you keep explaining these plays over and over to them, and keep quizzing them, eventually they will re-member them. All players, except the goalkeeper, need to learn these plays.

Drill No. 84- Defensive Techniques and Tactics

The Basics are:

Until the kickoff is made, all defensive players have to be at least 10 yards away from the ball. What the defense basically wants to do is, try to recover the ball just as soon as the kick-off is made. Here is a good attack play right off the kickoff. Two center forwards (F1 & F2) play 10 yards away, right up on the edges of the center circle. What they try to do is go right at, and con-verge on P2 when P1 passes the ball to that player *(SEE FIGURE 109)*. This really disrupts play and sometimes re-sults in intercepting the ball. This would actually be option No. 2 though.

Usually though, at youth level

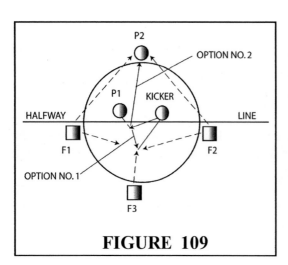

FIGURE 109

soccer, the kicker passes the ball to P1, who passes it back to them. When this happens, the two center forwards (F1 & F2) converge on the kicker *(SEE FIGURE 109)*. This would be option No. 1.

Another defensive play would be to surprise the kickoff team and put a forward (F3) right out in front of the kicker 10 yards. That players job is to go right at the kicker and attempt to block, tackle, or recover the ball as quickly after the kick as possible. This would be option No. 3. However, any one of these three plays could be a problem though because some lower level youth soccer leagues will not let you use this pressing tactic. They want kids to learn how to move the ball from the kickoff. If this is the case in your league, then move F1 and F2 straight back 10 yards, in line, and apply the pressure the same way.

Drills for Defending and Marking

Defending

Defense is sometimes what wins games. Young kids need to start right out and learn defense, even before they get to their first team. Defenders have to be smart because they have to be in the right place, at the right time, to stop attackers. They have to be quick, to move to different parts of the field. They have to learn how to steal the ball *(SEE THE SECTION ON STEALING)*. They must learn how to tackle, to take the ball away from an advancing player *(SEE THE SECTION ON TACKLING)*. And sometimes they even have to block shots on goal just like the goalkeeper. When I say that though, they **_can not_** use their hands and arms like the goalkeeper. They have to do it with their feet. As an example, instead of diving for the ball hands first, they would have to slide or dive with the feet *(SEE FIGURE 65)*. They have to learn how to come up and challenge attacking players, instead of standing there and waiting for the attacking player to come to them. What happens many times when they wait is, the attacking players momentum takes them right around your son or daughter for a clear shot on goal. And when they come up to challenge, **_always watch the ball and not the opponents feet or eyes._**

Timing is critical for defenders because if they go down on a slide tackle and miss, the attacking player probably has a clear shot on goal. The rule for kids should be, don't go down on the ground for a tackle if no one is behind you to back you up. So explain to your son or daughter, they have to always be aware of where their defending team mates are on the field.

Drill No. 85- Ball and Cover Tactic

The Basics are:

This is a defensive strategy where two defenders cover an attacking player, like maybe the opposing teams best player. How this works is, one player (ball) guards the ball, and the second defender (cover) gets in a position to close off the passing lane towards the center of the field. This tactic allows the defender guarding the ball to be more aggressive and challenge the attacking player with the ball. And the second defender is then in a good position to steal any attempted passes.

Practice:

To practice this tactic you, mom or dad, will need to get one of your son or daughters friends or a helper (as an opponent). Then find a large backyard or grassy area. Then, mom or dad, go out to a spot about 10 yards in front of them. Start dribbling the ball towards them. Have them face you, with the friend or helper about 2 yards away and to the side of them *(SEE FIGURE 110)*. When you are about 4 yards away, kick pass the ball to your left and right in front of the helper. Your son or daughter should come right at you and attempt to steal the ball, or kick it away towards the side away from the helper. If you get the pass away, in front of the helper, your son or daughter has to come up and clear out the ball, by kicking it straight ahead of them. Also try this by reversing the tactic, and kick passing the ball to the other side. Have your son or daughter practice both the ball, and the cover positions. For the skills they need, *SEE THE SEC-TIONS ON BLOCKING & TACKLING, TRAPPING & RECEIVING, KICKING & SHOOTING, and VOLLEY-ING*. All defenders, center backs, and fullbacks, need to work on these drills and tactics.

FIGURE 110

Drill No. 86- Clearing

The Basics are:

Clearing is getting the ball out of bounds, or moving it quickly back down towards the opponents goal, after you have intercepted it. Defenders should try and keep the advancing ball way out to the outside of the field if possible. All but one, in the line of the defenders, should be challenging the attacker and playing the ball out to the sides of the field while that one player stays back in the middle of the field. This is to eject and clear out any cross shots, or passes, by the opposing team.

Practice:

The practice technique for clearing the ball can be set up the same way as for "ball and cover" practice. Except you don't need the helper. When they play the part of the outside defender, they clear the ball out by stealing it or kicking it away from you towards the sides. When they play the part of the center defender, they clear the ball out by kicking it straight ahead as hard as they can. For the skills they need, *SEE THE SECTIONS ON BLOCKING & TACKLING, TRAPPING & RECEIVING, KICKING & SHOOTING, and VOLLEYING*. All defenders, center backs, and fullbacks, need to work on these drills and tactics.

Drill No. 87- Marking

The Basics are:

Marking is really just closely watching, or guarding, an opposing player by staying right with them *(SEE FIGURE 111)*. However there is "one on one" marking, and there is "zone" marking. One on one marking might be when the attacking player with the ball comes into your area, or it might be you have been told to mark the opposing teams best player. Zone marking is almost the same, except if

FIGURE 111

either of these types of players enter your area on the field then leaves toward the other side of the field, you don't move with them. Watch them, but stay in your zone.

To mark an opposing player, you need to always keep your feet moving so you can react to any move they make. When they are about a yard away, you need to shuffle or slide sideways, always keeping yourself between them and the goal. Then just at the right moment, like if they slow down a bit, go in for the steal, block, or tackle. That moment should be just when the opponent lets the ball bounce off their foot *(SEE FIGURE 111)*. Come into the opponent from the side of your strong leg, not from the front. It's to your advantage because you are forcing them to go to only one side, not either side. One more thing to point out when there is more than one player breaking and coming right at you, move back and go into a delaying tactic until your team mates get there to help. For the skills they need, ***SEE THE SECTIONS ON BLOCKING & TACKLING, TRAPPING & RECEIVING, KICKING & SHOOTING, and VOLLEYING*** .

Practice:

To practice this tactic you, mom or dad, will need to get one of your son or daughters friends as a helper (the opponent). Then find a large backyard or grassy area. Then, mom or dad, have the helper go out to a spot about 10 yards in front of them. Have them start dribbling the ball towards your son or daughter. Have your son or daughter face the helper, and have them stay right with them when they get a yard or two away. They want to have their strong foot on the same side the helper is dribbling on. First have them slide side ways, and force the helper to move to where the outside of the field would be. Have them keep doing this for awhile, except sometimes have the helper almost stop, so they can go for the steal or a tackle. You can just sit down and explain to them how the "one on one", and the "zone, marking works. All players, except goalkeepers, need to learn these tactics and techniques. This is because when they go from offense to defense, it will help them become a good defender.

Formations

It would be good if all young boys and girls playing Youth Soccer, knew their basic formations. And generally where all the different players are located within that formation. This way it will save the coaches some time explaining the general formation, and how it works, during practice. And it will let the coaches spend a little more time on the techniques of the individual players.

What I am going to do is, show some of the more common basic formations that might be used in Youth Soccer. At least your son or daughter can see, and learn, some of the different alignments that are popular. These formations change from offense to defense, depending on who has the ball. Most of the time this is the way they will line up just after the kickoff. And many times coaches will substitute more forwards when they want more offensive scoring. Or they might substitute more defenders, to stop the opposition from scoring too many goals.

Offensive and Defensive Player ID's

Symbol	Description	Symbol	Description
G	Goalkeeper	LWB	Left Wingback
F	Forward	RWB	Right Wingback
CF	Center Forward	SW	Sweeper
M	Midfielder	CD	Center Defenders (Stoppers)
LM	Left Midfielder	RB	Right Back (Fullback)
RM	Right Midfielder	LW	Left Wing
LB	Left Back (Fullback)	RW	Right Wing
CB	Center Back		

COMMON FORMATIONS

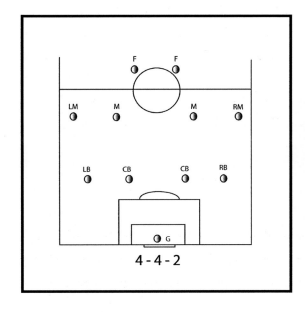

4 - 4 - 2

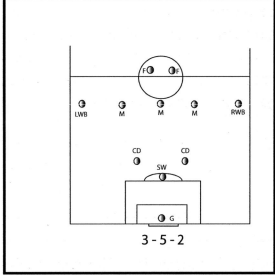

3 - 5 - 2

COMMON FORMATIONS

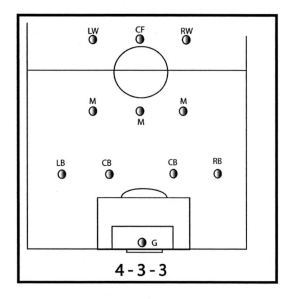

4 - 3 - 3

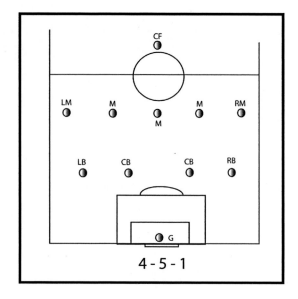

4 - 5 - 1

New Parent Orientation

The Game of Soccer

This section is for those mom and dads that may not know much about the game of soccer, or how it is played. The game is basically divided into two phases. They are offensive soccer, and defensive soccer. The team that scores the most points (goals) wins the game.

There are two different types of games. First there is the outdoor, on grass, 11 players, game we all see and hear about. Then there is the "Short Sided" game that most people probably never even heard of. Short sided games are played with fewer players (3-9), smaller field sizes, shorter time periods, smaller balls, and more playing time per player. The "short sided game" developed to help the younger kids learn the game, without so many players and all the confusion. There are fewer players on a team so they learn more, and do it at a faster pace because the coaches can concentrate and focus on the teaching. The rules are less restrictive so that the kids have more fun. Because there are fewer players, it encourages players to move without the ball, and find open spaces to get passes. Some of the best players in the world got their start playing short sided soccer. The youngest kids (U6) play on a field about the size of a basketball court. In the section on "the playing field ", you will find a chart *(SEE FIGURE*

113) with the official AYSO (American Youth Soccer Organization) field sizes for the different "short sided soccer" age groups. Also in the section on "equipment", you will find a chart *(SEE FIGURE 119)* with the ball sizes for all soccer age groups. For the time or duration of a game, for all levels, *SEE FIGURE 114.*

Offensive Game

The Scoring

When the team is in the offensive phase, the object is to score points. A goal is scored when the entire ball passes the goal line between the goal posts, and under the crossbar. Each goal counts as 1 point. However, it only counts if the ball *has not* been thrown, carried, or propelled, by the hand or arm of the offensive player. One goal counts as one point. In the case of a forfeited game, the score is 1-0 in favor of the non offending team. The players on the field are on offense when one of the players on your team has control of the ball. If one of the players on the opposing team intercepts the ball, and they have control of the ball, your team immediately goes from offense to defense. The key word is control. With young youth soccer teams, the ball can go back and forth between players in a matter of seconds.

How Goals are Scored

There are many ways a goal can be scored. They are the same for the regular outdoor game and the short sided game. The most common way is when one or more offensive players combine, on an attacking play, to kick the ball into the goal. A player may kick the ball in directly from a kickoff. This is very hard to do, especially in youth soccer. First it is a long way for small young kids to kick the ball. And the goalkeeper would have a good chance to catch it, especially since it would be going much slower when it get to them. A goal may be scored from a direct free kick. This is where the player making the kick gets it directly past the goal keeper, defenders, and into the goal. A goal may be scored from a penalty kick. This is where the player making the kick also gets it past the goalkeeper, one on one, from the penalty arc area. A goal may be scored directly from a corner kick. This is where the player making the kick can make a bending curving kick, all the way, directly into the goal. A goal may be scored on a dropped ball. This is when one of two players directly kicks a ball into the goal, from a dropped ball by an official. The ball has to hit the ground though before either player can kick it. A goal may be scored from a direct throw, punt, or drop kick. This is when the goalkeeper distributes the ball out from the goal area, and it goes directly into the opponents goal. Probably not likely with kids.

What the Offense does

Play starts with both teams lining up, opposing each other, for an opening kickoff. The team that wins the coin toss before the game starts, gets to pick which goal it will attack for the first half. The other team gets to kick off. Which usually means they go on offense. In the second half of the game they switch sides, and the team that won the coin toss before the game started, gets to kick off. The team making the kick off has a player assigned to make the kick off. That player is usually one of their best forwards. Play starts when the ball is placed on the center mark, and the assigned player kicks the ball forward. What they usually do is, make a short sideways kick right out in front of either the player to their right, or to their left. Then that player taps the ball right back to the kicker *(SEE FIGURE 108)*. That player then begins to dribble the ball down the field towards the goal. Just before the kick off, the opposing team lines up their front line forward defending players 10 yards away from the ball, which has been placed at the halfway line center circle. Once play has started, the offense dribbles, or passes the ball down towards their goal. They keep doing this until they either make a goal, or they lose control of the ball. When they lose control of the ball they immediately switch to defense. The other team then goes on offense, and counter attacks.

Offensive Team Members

The offensive team can have 11 players on their side of the field. The team can have one goalkeeper, and 10 other players. Depending on the formation they are in, they can be defenders, midfielders, and forward players. Or they can be different combinations of these players. Such as sweepers, center defenders, backs, wings, wingbacks, and strikers *(SEE THE SECTION ON FORMATIONS)*.

What Offensive Players do

Forwards are players that can score goals. Usually the best player on the team is a forward. A special forward, called a striker, is there to attack quickly and shoot for goals. Forwards usually make the kick off. When they get the ball back after the kick off, their job is to move upfield and get in position to kick a goal. They can pass the ball off and move into position, or they can dribble towards the goal. Center forwards stay right around the middle of the field, and basically look for quick shots on goal right up the middle. Left wings, and right wings, play on either side of the center forward. They are called wings because the stay mostly out on the sides (wings) of the field, and look for chances to make shots on goal. Midfielders back up the forwards, keep control of the ball, and make passes to open players. Center midfielders stay right near the middle of the field, to stop short "break away's" up the middle of the field.

Left wingbacks, and right wingbacks, stay out to the sides of the midfielders group. These are special midfielders that are fast, good defenders, good blocker's and tacklers. Also they can go up the sides (wings) of the field and score goals quickly on counter attacks if necessary. If the opposition gains control of the ball, they move back to help the defenders. Good midfielders control the game by keeping the ball, and the flow of play going towards their goal. They have to be good tacklers when the opposing team has the ball. They also have to be in good shape physically because they have to do the most running. Defenders, center defenders, left backs, right backs, and center backs, stay back near their goal. They support the attack, and try to intercept counter attack passes, or kicks on goal. If they get the ball back, they try to get it back upfield to one of their midfielders, or forwards as quickly as possible. Fullbacks are really either left backs or right backs. But they have a special job. That is to make long dribbling runs all the way up the sideline, or flanks, after receiving or intercepting the ball. To do this they should be big and strong, thus the name fullback as in football.

Defensive Game

Defensive Scoring
Technically a defender could score a goal. It's very unlikely though, especially with kids because they would have to be on defense, and intercept a pass or kick, then kick or dribble the ball directly into the goal. Even that description is a stretch. And the moment they intercept the ball, they are technically on offense anyway. So I guess it all depends on how you look at it. Basically the defense is there to stop scoring, not to score points.

What the Defense does
The object of the defense is to stop the other team from scoring. They usually have a row of players that stay back, and behind the play upfield, to help the goalkeeper defend the goal. This row of defenders may have left backs, center backs, right backs, or center defenders (stoppers). The sweeper stays right in front of the goalkeeper. The goalkeeper stays right in the goal area most of the time, to stop the ball from getting through.

What Defensive Players do

A sweeper stays back right in the front of the penalty area. Their job is to be a last chance defender. They pick up any unmarked player breaking into the goal area. And they intercept any balls that get behind the defense. Stoppers (center defenders) are just that. They are there to stop players from dribbling in, and making shots on goal. They, along with the sweeper, are your best defenders. They mark the opposing teams best forwards. Center backs, left backs, and right backs, are defenders. Their job is to stop any opposing team players trying to break through towards the goal. Wings play up in front with the forwards. In most cases they play out to the outside of the field. They are like forwards, except when the opposing team takes control of the ball. Then they fall back and try to stop counter attacks. Wingbacks are on the outside of the midfielders group. They stop attacking players along the side line. And if they recover the ball, they start a counter attack up the field and get the ball to the forwards. The goalkeeper stays in the goal area. Their job is to stop the ball from going into the goal. The goal keeper is usually one of the best players on the team. They have to be very quick, and smart, to stop the opposing team from scoring goals. And they have to be able clear the ball, way up field, after they recover it.

Defensive Team Members

When on defense, the team can have 11 players on the field. The goalkeeper defends the goal. The rest of the 10 players will depend on what defensive formation the coach wants to use, and what the opposing team likes to do on offense. Usually there are 4 players that stay back in a line, they are called defenders. They make up what is referred to as a 4-4-2 (the most popular) formation. There are two other common versions of this defense. They are the 4-3-3 formation, and the 4-5-1 formation *(See the section on Formations)*. The line of 4 players is usually made up of 2 center backs, a left back, and a right back.

On teams, that are very defensive minded, there might be 2 center defenders (stoppers), and a sweeper, that stay back for defensive purposes. This is called a 3-5-2 formation *(See the section on Formations)*. The players that are up in front, when the team is on defense, are usually forwards, strikers, and wings in the front line, with midfielders and wingbacks in the middle line. The midfielders fall back, and help the defenders when the team is on defense. The forwards usually stay up in front when the team is on defense. They try to recover the ball, if they can while the opposing team has the ball in the opposing teams half of the field. When the ball crosses over midfield, to the offensive teams half of the field, they stay back so they are up front and ready when the counter attack starts.

The Playing Field

The overall playing field size for professional soccer, college, and high school is 100 to 120 yards long by 55 to 75 yards wide *(SEE FIGURE 112)*. There are goals located at each end of the field. They are placed on the goal lines, or end lines part of the field. They have two posts that are 8 yards apart, with a crossbar 8 feet high. Nets are attached to the posts and crossbar, and they are fastened to ground behind the goal. They are centered within the width of the field. Most youth teams, playing outside on grass, play on the same size field as the high school teams.

There are team areas, and benches, located on one side of the field near mid field. There is an officials area right in the middle of that side of the field, then the home team area is one side of the officials area, and the opposing team area is on the other side. Just coaches and players are allowed in the team area. Spectators are on the opposite side of the field away from the players.

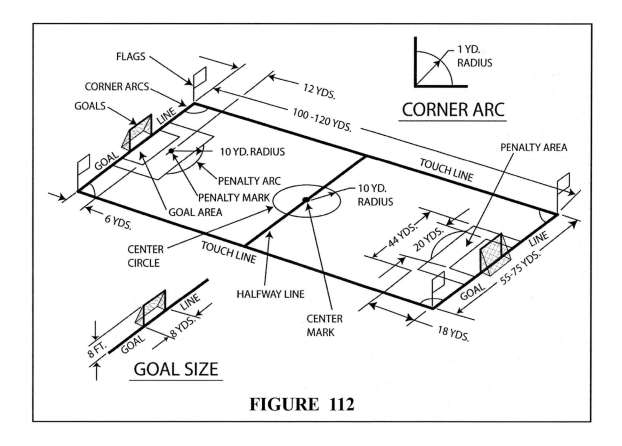

FIGURE 112

There are teams around the USA that play the "short sided" game. Those field sizes vary for the younger age groups *(SEE FIGURE 113)*. Except for the overall dimensions, the other field marking is similar to a regular field. There are exceptions though. In the U6 age group, no distinctive lines are required inside the field boundary. Cones may be used to mark the field. This is all that is required for the 6 year olds *(SEE FIGURE 113)*. The whole idea is just let them play. For U8 short sided soccer, the field changes a little. It grows in size, and there is a halfway line and a center circle. The goals, and the goal area, are smaller than regular size. And the corners have corner arcs *(SEE FIGURE 113)*. For U10 short sided soccer, all the field markings are there except they are down sized

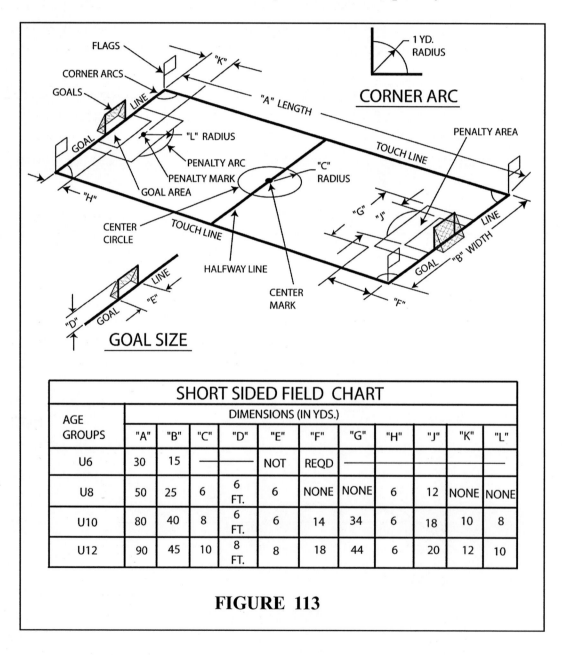

SHORT SIDED FIELD CHART

AGE GROUPS	DIMENSIONS (IN YDS.)										
	"A"	"B"	"C"	"D"	"E"	"F"	"G"	"H"	"J"	"K"	"L"
U6	30	15	———	———	NOT	REQD	———	———	———	———	———
U8	50	25	6	6 FT.	6	NONE	NONE	6	12	NONE	NONE
U10	80	40	8	6 FT.	6	14	34	6	18	10	8
U12	90	45	10	8 FT.	8	18	44	6	20	12	10

FIGURE 113

(SEE FIGURE 113). For U12 short sided soccer, all the field markings are the same size as a regular soccer field, except the overall field size is still smaller than a regular size field *(SEE FIGURE 113)*.

U6 represents the 6 and 7 year olds. U8 represents the 8 and 9 year olds. U10 represents the 10 and 11 year olds. U12 represents 12 and 13 year olds.

General Game Rules

The game of soccer is divided into two halves of time. In some leagues there is a quarter break in play, to make substitutions. Between halves there is a half time break. Around the USA the time intervals for a soccer game may vary. You almost have to check with the league you are in, to get the correct information for your area of the country. The information I am providing on time intervals comes from the general St. Louis, Missouri area *(SEE FIGURE 114)*. And it basically covers youth soccer up to High School. Much of the information in this book comes from the "CYC" (Catholic Youth Council) leagues which make up

TIME INTERVAL PER HALF vs AGE GROUPS			
AGE GROUPS	TIME INTERVAL (MINUTES)		
"CYC"	FIRST HALF	HALF TIME	SECOND HALF
ATOM MINOR	DISTRICT DISCRETION	5	DISTRICT DISCRETION
ATOM MAJOR	DISTRICT DISCRETION	5	DISTRICT DISCRETION
BANTAM MINOR	25	5	25
BANTAM MAJOR	25	5	25
MIDGET	30	5	30
CRUSADER	30	5	30
CADET	35	5	35
INTERMEDIATE	35	5	35
PAROCHIAL	35	5	35
"AYSO"			
U6	10	5 - 10	10
U8	20	5 - 10	20
U10	25	5 - 10	25
U12	30	5 - 10	30
U14	35	5 - 10	35

FIGURE 114

many teams in the St. Louis area. How long they play depends on the age group they play in.

The "CYC" breaks into divisions. They are:
1. Atom Minor, 1st grade (7) boys and girls.
2. Atom Major, 2nd grade (8) boys and girls.
3. Bantam Minor, 3rd grade (9) boys and girls.
4. Bantam Major, 4th grade (10) boys and girls.
5. Midget, 5th grade (11) boys and girls.
6. Crusader, 6th grade (12) boys and girls.
7. Cadet, 7th grade (13) boys and girls.
8. Intermediate, 8th grade (14) boys and girls.
9. Parochial, 8th grade (14) boys and girls.

By comparison the "AYSO" (American Youth Soccer Organization) breaks into age groups. They are:
1. U6, 6 and 7 year olds.
2. U8, 8 and 9 year olds.
3. U10, 10 and 11 year olds.
4. U12, 12 and 13 year olds.
5. U14, 14 and 15 year olds.

There are different soccer ball sizes used in the different divisions, and age groups *(SEE SECTION ON EQUIPMENT)*. There is a chart in the equipment section of this book, showing the relationship between age groups's and ball sizes. The ball has to be spherical, and made of leather or other suitable material. Also they may be coated in plastic, to prevent water absorption in wet conditions. The ball is usually white in color, so it can be seen on the grass, and at night. Some balls have dark colored lines, or alternating solid color panels, on them.

There is a kickoff at the start of the game at the center mark of the field *(SEE THE SECTION ON THE KICKOFF)*. After half time there is another kickoff at the center mark on the field. There is a coin toss before the game to see which team defends which goal, and which team kicks off.

The game then proceeds, with the team in control of the ball attacking and attempting to score a goal. There are many strategies and tactics teams will use to score goals. I am not going into them in this book because there are too many to list. You could write an entire book on just tactics, and strategies, used around the world in soccer.

To help identify the players, the jersey's (shirts) have a large number on the back. Each team usually has a contrasting color jersey, to distinguish one teams players from the other teams players *(SEE SECTION ON EQUIPMENT)*.

There are many rules and penalties in the game, that present scoring opportunities. Some of them are discussed in the *"Referee's and Penalties"*. *Section* of the book. Others are discussed in different sections of the book. For serious rules violations, there are cards given by the referee. As an example, getting a "red card" can lead to ejection from the game.

The players uniform, and the equipment, they wear have rules *(SEE THE SECTION ON EQUIPMENT)*. There are rules for when the ball is in or out of play. The entire ball must cross the touch line or goal line, to be out of play. If the game is tied at the end of regular play, there are rules for an overtime period to come up with a winner. It could be a penalty shoot out, or a "sudden (death) victory" procedure (knock out competition), depending on whichever the league decides. As an example, two 15 minute "sudden victory" periods can be played to settle the tie. The first team to score a goal in either of these periods, wins the game. A coin flip will decide the choice of goals for the first period, the loser kicks off. If a second period is needed, the teams change goals and which team kicks off. If the game is still tied after the two 15 minute periods, penalty kicks *(SEE SECTION ON PENALTY KICKS, PAGE 100)* will be used to decide the winner (knock out competition). Each team would take 5 penalty kicks. The referee chooses the goal. There is a coin toss to see which team kicks first. They would take turns alternating until each team has their 5 kicks. Whichever team scores the most penalty kicks wins the game. If each scores an equal number of penalty kicks at the end of their 5 kicks, they continue taking penalty kicks back and forth until one team misses. The other team then wins the game.

There are rules for "off sides" during the game. These rules are complicated for most people to understand *(SEE SECTION ON REFEREE'S & PENALTIES)*. There will be illustrations there to illustrate some examples of off sides. These are rules to keep one team from having an unfair advantage, for scoring a goal. An example of an unfair advantage would be, to have one or more players stand around the goal area and wait for a quick pass to them. The opposing players might all be way down towards the other end of the field, and could not get back in time to defend the goal. Thus an easy goal could be scored by the attacking team.

Players can be substituted during the game. However there are rules for substitutions. A substitute player can go on the field during a stoppage in the game. However they must have the referee's permission, and it has to be after the player being replaced has left the field. To assure that all kids get into the game, the referee is required to stop the game midway through each half, at a convenient stopping point, to allow substitutions. Substitutions for injury may be made at any time. If you lose a player because of a red card, you do not get to substitute for them. You play with a player short for the rest of the game.

When the ball goes out of bounds across the side "touch lines", there is a throw in *(SEE THE SECTION ON THROWING)*. The team of the player that last touched the ball before it went out of bounds, loses the ball to the opposing team. The opposing team then gets to make a "throw in" to one of their own players. If they miss getting the ball to their own team mate, the opposing team can intercept the ball and go on the attack again.

When there is a temporary stoppage, the referee drops the ball to restart the game. This is where he drops the ball, between two opposing players, close to where the stoppage occurred. Play starts again as soon as the ball hits the ground, with one of the two players kicking the ball or taking control for their team. The team with control of the ball then goes on the attack towards the goal.

When the ball is kicked by the offensive team out of bounds over the goal line, but not into the goal, the defending team gets a goal kick *(SEE GOAL KICKS, PAGE 111)* if the attacking team last touched the ball. The defending team then puts the ball down on the ground anywhere in the goal area. Then one of the players, or the goalkeeper, kicks the ball down field as far as they can, to keep it away from the goal area. The ball is not in play though until it is kicked out of, or clears, the penalty area.

When the ball is kicked out of bounds over the goal line by the defending team, the attacking team gets to make a corner kick *(SEE THE SECTION ON SHOOTING & KICKING GOALS)*. This is where the player puts the ball down in the corner of the field circle, nearest where the ball went out of bounds, then kicks the ball towards the goal or to a team mate.

Referee's and Penalties

Why have Referee's
I think that's very obvious, without them the game could get real ugly, fights, people getting hurt, fan rioting, and who knows what else could happen. Soccer games have referee's, to judge whether the rules have been followed. The game of soccer is more complicated than you might think, and that is why we need referee's to keep track of the rules. All levels of soccer teams, except youth soccer teams, have a head referee and two assistant referee's. Youth soccer

games may only have one referee. Or they may have a head referee and one assistant referee. This is because in some leagues it is hard to get anyone to volunteer, to be a referee. And I think it's mostly because fans, and parents, don't want to be the one hollered at if they are the referee making the call. And then some of the fans, friends, or other parents watching don't like the call and will get mad at them. And I think that too few referee's has a lot to do with people getting mad at games. Too few referee's are not able to see every rule infraction that occurs on the field. It's a lot easier to watch for infractions of the rules when you have 3 referee's present all during the game. So please try to be tolerant of the situation as parents while you are watching your son or daughter's game. I have been at youth sports games where one of the two officials (referee's) got sick and had to leave. Now you have only one referee, and the teams were left with the decision of whether to play the game with one official or not at all. Because the game was at the lowest level of teams in the league, and late in the season with no championship on the line, both teams agreed to go with one official. And he had a very tough job, believe me. A good game for a referee is a quiet game. This means he was unnoticed, and did his job.

When an infraction of the rules occurs, either the referee or the assistant referee will make the call. Or in some cases both. If the assistant referee and the head referee do not agree on the call, the head referee's decision is final. The referee will make calls by blowing his whistle, and making a hand signal, indicating the infraction or foul. In some cases the referee may have to blow the whistle a second time to make their indication. The assistant referee will make calls using a flag. How they hold the flag indicates the infraction.

Who are the Officials

The head referee (HR) is in charge of the game. He makes the final decision in a 3 referee alignment. You will find head referee working on a diagonal path across the field *(SEE FIGURE 115)*. In the "dual officiating" system, there is a lead official and a trail

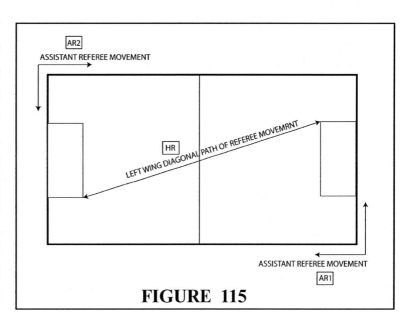

FIGURE 115

FIGURE 116

official. The head referee is the lead official. The head referee's runs the whole game basically. They make most of the calls, with help from the assistant referee's. They inspect the field before a game, they inspect the players, and they have a pregame talk with the players. They conduct the coin toss, and they keep track of the "time". They call fouls, and control penalties for the foul. They start and stop the game. They hold up a "yellow" or a "red" card if necessary. They declare the ball "ready for play" on corner kicks, penalty kicks, and free kicks.

The assistant referee indicates the direction of the throw in by bringing the flag up to a 45 degree angle in the direction of the throw in is to be taken.

During the taking of the throw in, the assistant referee looks for foot faults as outlined in rule 15.1.3.

The flag should not be brought across the body. Appropriately, the flag should not be switched to the alternate hand.

Throw In

Substitution

Corner Kick
Assistant referee should point to the nearest corner.

Goal Kick
Assistant referee should point to the goal area.

Stop Play - Offside
Assistant referee should indicate he/she has seen an offside.

Offside Free Kick
When referee stops play, assistant referee indicates position on the far side of the field.

Offside Free Kick
When referee stops play, assistant referee indicates position near center of field.

Offside Free Kick
When referee stops play, assistant referee indicates position on near side of field.

FIGURE 117

They verify the score, fill out the paper work, and bring in the flags when the game is over. When there is only one referee for the game, they work the center of the field diagonally because they can see the play better. For their signals *SEE FIGURE 116.*

In the two assistant referee system (AR1 & AR2), they work the two opposite corners of the field *(SEE FIGURE 115)*. In the one assistant referee system, they work on one corner, the head referee works the opposite corner.

The assistant referee (AR1) is the trail official on the play. They indicate their calls with "flags" *(SEE FIGURE 117)*. They declare the ball "ready for play" with a second whistle, at the start of each half, the kickoff after a goal, drop balls, and goal kicks. They indicate, when the ball is out of play, which team is entitled to the throw in, corner kicks, and goal kicks. They signal when a goal is scored. However, sometimes the head referee is in a better position and makes the call when a goal is scored. As the game is going on, they position themselves in line with second to last defender or the ball. This way they can watch for off sides violations. For their signals *SEE FIGURE 117*.

Referee's (officials) are easily recognized on the field by their uniform, which is usually a black shirt, shorts, shoes, and black stockings with white stripes. And if they need a contrasting color because the one of the teams is in black, they wear a bright red or yellow vest over their shirt. And they are usually adults, which makes them stand out bigger than the kids.

Penalties and Fouls

Penalties and fouls are called by the referee, and assistant referee's. We are not going to indicate every possible penalty or foul in this section. We will try to go over the ones you might normally see in a game.

Most of the penalties, and fouls, are called by the head referee. The assistant referee usually calls goals, out of bounds, and offsides. If the defending team player last touches the ball before it goes out of bounds, over the goal line, the attacking team wins a corner kick *(SEE PAGE 98)*, which gives them another way to try and score. When a attacking team player last touches the ball before it goes out of bounds, over the goal line, the defending team gets a goal kick. This is a way in which they can clear the ball way downfield. That delays the attacking teams attack plan.

There are two fouls that give the attacking team an advantage on scoring a goal. They are a "direct free kick" *(SEE PAGE 94)*, and an "indirect free kick" *(SEE PAGE 96)*.

Fouls that result in a direct free kick are called penal fouls. Only the kicker has to touch the ball, in a direct free kick, in order for a goal to be scored.

Fouls that give a team a direct free kick are:
- Kicking or attempting to kick an opponent.
- Striking or attempting to strike an opponent .
- Pushing, charging, tripping and attempting to trip, holding, or jumping at an opponent.

138

- When tackling an opponent, and making contact with the opponent instead of the ball.
- Players, except the goalkeeper, deliberately handling the ball in their own penalty area.
- Displaying unsportsmanlike conduct such as spitting, or cursing, at an opponent.

Direct free kicks are taken from where the foul occurred. If any of the above fouls are committed by a player, inside their own penalty area, a "penalty kick" is awarded to the other team *(SEE PAGE 100)*.

Fouls that result in an indirect free kick are called non-penal fouls. The kicker and at least one other player, of either team, has to touch the ball before a goal can be scored.

Fouls that give a team an indirect free kick are:
- Dangerous play, such as high kicking around another players head, and trying to play a ball held by the goalkeeper.
- Getting between an opponent and the ball, when not playing the ball.
- Keeping the goalkeeper from playing the ball, by having excessive contact with them while in the penalty area.
- The goalkeeper having possession of the ball longer than 6 seconds within the penalty area. Or they attempt to control the ball with their hands when the ball was last kicked to them (not headed to them, or after it was thrown in directly to them) by a team mate.

There are two kinds of misconduct, those for which a player is ejected, and those for which a caution is given. First there is actions that result in a caution (yellow card), and second there is action that results in the player being ejected from the field. When given a second yellow card, it automatically results in a red card, and ejected from the game.

A player is shown a yellow card and cautioned for any of the following offenses:
- Displaying unsportsmanlike conduct.
- Showing dissent by actions or words.
- Constantly not following the rules of the game.
- Delaying the restart of play.
- Failing to keep the required distance when play is restarted with a corner kick or a free kick.
- Deliberately leaving the field, entering, or re-entering the field without the referee's permission.

- Tackling an opponent from behind.

A player is shown a red card, and is sent off the field for any of the following offenses:
- Committing serious foul play.
- Showing violent conduct.
- Spitting at an opponent or another person.
- Deliberately handling the ball to prevent a goal, or an obvious goal, scoring chance by the opposing team (except the goalkeeper in their own penalty area).
- Fouling an opponent, who is moving toward the goal and has an obvious chance to score.
- Using insulting, offensive, or abusive, language or gestures.
- Getting a second yellow card in the same game.

Offsides is one of the more complicated of the soccer rules for most people to understand. What you must understand as a parent is, if not called it can be an unfair advantage for the attacking team. Generally speaking it means a player can not hang way back upfield on the opponents side when the play is going on way down in their end of the field, and wait for a counter attack quick pass back to them. I am sure offside is very hard for the referee's to see sometimes, especially with the players all bunched up around the ball. What the rule basically says is, a player is ruled to be in an offside position if they are ahead of the ball in the opponents half of the field when the ball is passed to them. That is **_unless_** at least two opponents (usually a player and the goalkeeper) are between them and the opponents goal line. Also there can be **_no offside_** directly from a throw in, a goal kick, a corner kick, or when the player is in their half of the field.

Even after all of the above being said, the referee shall not call offside on a player when the player in that position is not involved in an active play, is not interfering with an opponent, is not interfering with a play, or is not trying to take an advantage by being in that position. In some of the other upper division games, a team will set up a player for an "offside trap". This would be when they see a player is kind of hanging way back, on their side of the field, then all the nearby players suddenly move away from that player in the opposite direction. This leaves the player offside with no one between them and the goalkeeper. When offside is called on a player, the penalty is an "indirect free kick" *(SEE PAGE 94)* for the other team, from the spot of the infraction . For some diagramed examples of offside, *SEE FIGURE 118.*

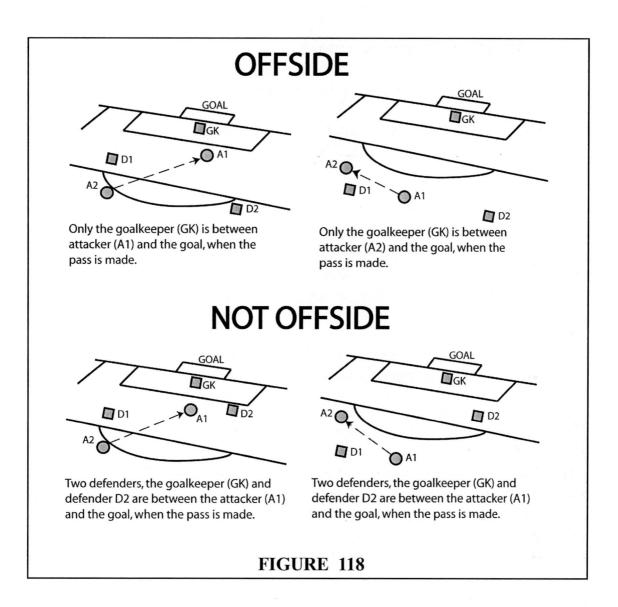

FIGURE 118

Soccer Terminology

All parents and kids should learn the terminology associated with soccer. This way they will understand what the coaches are talking about.

Ball, Soccer: This the ball the game will be played with. It is round in shape, and lighter in weight than a basketball. They come in many sizes. See Figure 119 for the different sizes used by the different organizations.

Bicycle Kick: This is a specialized kick where the player falls backwards just when a high pass comes into them, and turning almost upside down, they kick the ball over their head and behind them.

Break Away: This is usually when a forward, striker, or wing, breaks away from defenders around them and charges the goal, and goes one on one with the goalkeeper. This gives the player a good chance to score a goal.

Center Back: See "Fullbacks".

Center Circle: This is a 20 yard diameter circle right in the center of the field, with it's center a 10 yard radius from the field center mark. For kids under 12 years old, it is a slightly smaller diameter (See Figure 113).

Center Line: This is a line in the middle of the field that divides the field exactly in half. This line is parallel to the goal lines.

Center Mark (Spot): This is a 9 inch diameter spot mark right at the center of the field, from both directions. It is where the 10 yard radius for the center circle is drawn.

Center Pass: This is when the ball is passed to the center part of the field right in front of the goal. This gives a players team mates a better chance to score than from way out to the sideline.

Charge: This is shoulder bumping or jarring an opponent with the ball. It is legal so long as the player is playing the ball when contact with the ball carrier is made. And so long as there is no arm contact with the ball carrier. It's a judgement call by the referee, who determines whether the contact was too hard or dangerous to the ball carrier. If it was, he awards a free kick.

Chipping: This is when a player kicks a ball rolling on the ground where they kick the ball up in the air, in a looping manor, over the head of a defender in front of them.

Clearing the Ball: This is a defensive type kick, usually by a defender, way down the field away from the goal area. It is not necessarily to a team mate, but basically just to keep it away from the opponents getting a shot on goal.

Coin Toss: The referee flips a coin just before the game starts. The winner of the coin toss chooses whether to kick off or defend a particular goal. Sometimes choosing the upwind goal is a better choice than kicking the ball. Especially if the wind is strong at the time of the coin toss because it is an advantage to get the ball up field quicker and with more distance to the kicks.

Corner Kick: Whenever a ball, last touched by a defensive player, goes out of bounds past the goal line, the opponent is awarded a free direct kick. The ball is then placed in the pie shaped area in the corner of the field, nearest to where the ball went out of bounds. Then a player from the opponents team kicks the ball from the pie shaped area, and tries to place the kick right in front of the goal where a team mate attempts to head it, or kick it, into the goal for a score. The kicker can also try to make a bending type kick that goes directly into the goal. The defensive team players usually bunch up near the end of the goal in an attempt to block the kickers shot. The goalkeeper has to make the decision whether to knock the ball away, or attempt to jump way up and grab the ball in the air.

Cruyff Turn: This is a fake kicking move while dribbling, named after the famous Dutch soccer player, Johan Cruyff. You pretend to kick the ball, then with some clever foot moves, you turn and dribble off away from a defender.

Dead Ball Kick: This is a stationary kick where the referee has given a free kick to a team, on a penalty, and has placed the ball on the ground at a point near where the penalty occurred.

Dink: This is a little soft chip shot on goal, up and over a charging goalkeepers head. This is a really a volleyball term, used for a fake spike and dump shot over a blocker.

Direct Free Kick: When there is a penalty, the referee decides whether the kick is a direct or an indirect kick. For a direct kick it means the kicker can attempt to score a goal by shooting directly at the goal, without kicking it to a team mate first as in a indirect kick.

Distributing: This is when the goalkeeper makes a save by catching the ball. They then have 6 seconds to throw, roll, or kick, the ball out of the penalty area. It's usually to a team mate, but it can be just way down the field.

Drag Back Turn: This is a fake kicking move while dribbling where you pretend to kick the ball. Then as the foot goes over the top of the ball on the leg swing, it drags back over the top of the ball, and moves it backwards. Next with some clever foot moves, you turn and dribble off away from a defender.

Dribbling: This is when a player is moving the ball up or across the field, using little short kicks in front of them with their feet.

Drop Ball: When the referee does not know who touched the ball last out of bounds, or after an injury during play, they begin play again with a drop ball. It's like a face off in Hockey. The referee drops the ball between two opposing players. Both players attempt to kick the ball to a team mate on their team. All the other players from each side must stay 10 yards away.

Far Post: Shooters must learn what this term means. To a shooter this means the goal post farthest away from the goalkeeper as they stand in the goal. This is where they have more room to score a goal.

Finish: Remember hearing the term "A kid can attack but can't finish". This means the player dribbling up field can't make the pass or the kick on goal while at a fast dribble.

Flags: At the four corners of the field there are 5 foot high flags that visually mark all the corners of the field.

Forwards: They are fast offensive players who can dribble, pass, and shoot while at full speed. They are sometimes called wings and strikers. They play up in the forward part of the field when their team is on offense.

Free Kicks: Direct kicks, indirect kicks, goal kicks, penalty kicks, and corner kicks, are all free kicks. One of the strategies on free kicks is, move quickly, and attempt to catch the defense off guard. A free kick means the team awarded the kick does not have lots of players right next to them trying to kick the ball away. There are different rules, for the kicker and the defense, depending on what the penalty was for.

Fouls: This is when a player violates the rules and a penalty is called. The penalty is assessed against the team of the player making the foul.

Fullbacks: These are usually big strong, aggressive, defensive players that stay more at the back of play and protect from counter attacks. They might also be called backs, wing backs, center backs, stoppers, or sweepers. As in football, they are usually tough and hard for a dribbler to charge around.

Give and Go: This is an offensive maneuver where a player is dribbling up the field, and a team mate runs up along side of the dribbling player. They make a short pass over to the team mate who pretend to dribble straight ahead. When the defender goes after the team mate, they make a quick pass back to the first player who then sprints past the defender. This is also sometimes called a "wall pass".

Goal Kick: This is when the ball is kicked out of bounds over the goal line, but not into the goal, by the offensive team. The defending team then gets to put the ball down on the ground anywhere in the goal area, and kick it way out away from the goal. Usually the goalkeeper makes this kick.

Goalkeeper: The goalkeeper is a defensive player that stands in, or out in front of, the goal and tries to keep the offensive team from getting the ball into the goal for a score. They wear a specially marked jersey that distinguishes them from the other players.

Halfbacks: See Midfielders.

Heading: This is when a player uses their head (usually the forehead) to pass, move the ball forward, or move it into the goal for a score.

Indirect Free Kick: When there is a penalty, the referee decides whether the kick is a direct or an indirect kick. The kick is taken from the spot of the foul. For a indirect kick it means that one other player, from either team, has to touch the ball after the kicker has made the first kick. The kicker can get a pass back to them from a team mate, and then attempt to score a goal by shooting directly at the goal.

Injuries: When a player gets injured on the field during play, and they are unable to play any more, the referee may stop play and let the injured player be examined. If the player can not recover, then a substitution is allowed. The other team is allowed possession when play starts back up.

Juggling: This is handling the ball with the feet, chest, head, and thighs, in an effort to control the ball, and keep it away from the opponent.

Kickoff's: This is when one team kicks off the ball from the center of the field, in the center circle. This occurs at the beginning of the game, after halftime, after each period, or after a goal has been scored. All players from the other team have to be at least 10 yards away from the ball and on their side of the centerline, and all players on the kickoff team have to remain on their side of the centerline until the ball has been kicked.

Linesmen: You do not usually see linesmen in a youth soccer game. They are also sometimes referred to as an "Assistant Referee". They will be up and down the sidelines with a flag, to indicate when the ball is out of play, which team makes the throw in, corner kicks, goal kicks, and offsides.

Marking: This is the act of defending (guarding) against an opposing player, by staying as close to them as possible, without fouling. This is very important when the opposing player gets down into your penalty area. In football and basketball this is referred to as "man-to-man" defense.

Match: This is the official name of the soccer game

Midfielders: They are players that usually play mainly in the middle third of the soccer field. They are players with lots of endurance for running. They are the "grunts", or "grinders", of a soccer team. They run all over the field, and have to be fast with good soccer skills. They are sometimes referred to as wing backs, side halfbacks, center halfbacks, left midfielders, or right midfielders.

Officials: They are the referee, assistant referee, or linesmen.

Offside: The rules basically say that a player is considered offside if they are ahead of the ball in the opponents half of the field when the ball is passed to them. That is unless at least two opponents (an opponent player and the goalkeeper) are between them and the opponents goal line. That being said, the referee is not supposed to call an offsides on a player when that player is not involved in an active play, is not interfering with an opponent, is not interfering with a play, or is not trying to gain an advantage by being where they are. It's a referee's judgement call.

Overlap: This is when a player moves past a team mate, with the idea they will receive a pass, to help advance the ball upfield or towards the goal.

Passing: This is the act of getting the ball to a team mate, usually using the feet, but sometimes using the head. This usually gets the ball upfield quicker than by dribbling.

Penalties: There are rules for the game of soccer. If you violate the rules, or foul an opposing player, a penalty is called. There are a number of ways a penalty may be assessed. The referee calls penalties. See the section on "Penalties and Fouls" in this book for a description of how they are assessed, and what they are called for.

Penalty Kicks: A penalty kick is awarded when a defensive player fouls an offensive player when the defensive player is in their own penalty area of the field. This usually results in a direct free kick for the offensive team. This is when only the kicker and the goalkeeper are allowed in the penalty area.

Penalty Shootout: In a game that goes into overtime, this is a way to come up with a winner. Each team takes 5 penalty kicks. They take turns alternating until each team has their 5 kicks. Whichever team makes the most penalty kick goals, wins the game. If they are each tied after the 5 kicks, they continue taking penalty kicks back and forth until one team misses. The other team wins the game.

Penetration: This is when a team gets deep into the opposing teams part of the field, in preparation for an attack on goal.

Pressure: A good defense will mark and pressure the ball carrier, any way they can that is allowable. Sometimes just running hard towards a ball carrier, with a menacing look, will cause the ball carrier to make a bad pass that a team mate can intercept.

Protecting: This is basically placing your body between the defender and the ball while dribbling or maneuvering so that the ball can't be stolen. This is sometimes referred to as "shielding".

Receiving: This is the act of getting a pass from a team mate, or trying to intercept a pass from an opposing player. It has to be with the feet or some part of the body. It can't be with the hands or arms as in football.

Red Card: When a player is shown a red card, they are ejected from the game and sent off the field. This is usually because of a serious foul, or violent and abusive behavior.

Referee: They are the head official, and they are in charge of the game. They get help from the assistant referee and linesmen, but they make the final decisions.

Run off the Ball: This is a player getting into position when they don't have the ball. What they do is run to an open space, or try to create open space by moving to where the opponents are not located.

Shin Guards: They are guards that fit around the shin part of the lower leg. What they do is protect the players lower leg from being kicked hard in the shin area by another player, or opponent. They are padded and can keep you from possibly getting a broken lower leg. They are not a required part of the uniform in some leagues, but they should be. They must be covered by knee high stockings.

Shoes: They are the most important part of the uniform. If a player does not have good shoes they could slip and fall, possibly hurting themselves. Get good shoes, they should have smooth ball control surfaces around the sides , and the instep part, of the shoe. Get soccer shoes with molded cleats, even the best are not real expensive, and they help the player keep from slipping when making quick changes in direction.

Shootout (Sudden Death): This is one method of breaking a tie game. This is when a team is given the ball outside of the penalty area, and their kicker has 5 seconds to score a goal. The goalkeeper can move any where they wish. Each team is given a 5 second shot to score after a coin toss. It's sudden death so the first team to score wins the game. There are other types of overtime shootouts, but this is the latest and quickest.

Small Sided Game: This is usually a practice game with 3 to 6 players on a side. The field usually runs sideways on the main field. There is no goalkeeper, and the goals are marked with cones about 6 feet apart, or with small practice goals. This way more little kids get to play in a game situation because you can have several small fields on the big field.

Square: This is a lateral (sideway) pass to a team mate.

Stealing: This is getting the ball away from a dribbling opponent by reaching around and kicking the ball away from them. This could also be by blocking the ball, making a slide or ground tackle and kicking it away, then getting control of the ball and dribbling away.

Stoppers (Center Defenders): They are specialized defenders that usually play in the center of the field. They have to be fast, good at blocking, and tackling (stealing the ball), ball carriers. They are there to stop the other team from break aways, or getting the ball into scoring range.

Strikers: These are special forward players that are fast, good ball handlers that can get away from defenders, and can strike quickly with a shot on goal.

Sweepers: A sweeper is a very tough, durable, and smart player, like a second goalkeeper. They usually play (defend) around the front and sides of the penalty kick area. Their job is to keep attackers from getting into position to make a kick on goal. They have to be very good at tackling and blocking.

Tackle: This is basically the act of stealing, or getting the ball away from an opponent. See "Stealing".

Through: This is a pass by a player through and around the defense into an open space, for a team mate to run into to receive.

Throw In: This is when a player stands on the side line (out of bounds) and makes a two handed overhead pass into a team mate, to continue play after an opposing player has last touched it before it went out of bounds.

Tie Breaker: There are rules to break a tie game. See "Penalty Shootout", and "Shootout (Sudden Death)".

Touch: One touch means the player receiving a pass, touches it and passes it on in a single touch. A double touch means the player traps the ball with the first touch, and immediately passes it on with the second touch.

Trap: This is a method of receiving a pass, or collecting a moving ball. This can be accomplished with the feet, chest, thighs, head, or the whole body.

Volley: This is a player kicking the ball while the ball is still in the air. A full volley kick is harder and goes farther. The kicker usually uses a "hip turn" type kick for the full volley. A half volley kick is similar to a full volley kick, except the player lets the ball bounce once before they make contact.

Wall: This is when defenders line up shoulder to shoulder, and form a wall to deflect free kicks from going into the goal for a score. Players can't use their hands, or even raise their arms, to deflect the ball.

Wingbacks: These are fast, good passers, and ball handlers that play along the middle sides (wings) of the field, usually right behind the forwards.

Wings: Wings is just another name for forwards. However when their job is to play up forward, but out more to the side lines (wing areas) rather than in the middle of the field, they are called wings.

Yellow Card: When a player is shown a yellow card, it means caution. When the same player is shown a second yellow card during the game, it is an automatic red card, and ejection from the game.

Zone Defense: This is really "zone marking". It is when the defense is set up to mark any opposing player coming into their area (zone) of the field. This is _not_ like "one- on- one" marking, where you follow a particular player wherever they go on the field. In other words this is zone guarding, not man to man guarding as in basketball.

Equipment

Each level of soccer, from professional to youth teams, has rules on what equipment can and can not be used. Mostly, this is to protect the players from injury. In this book we will talk about youth equipment. Most youth soccer organizations and leagues have very similar rules, to the higher level soccer teams. Since there is some contact in soccer, the players must be protected. Most of the protection is directed to the ankles and legs.

Worn Equipment

Uniform

Most youth soccer organization rule books require a jersey (shirt), shorts, stockings, shin guards, and approved footwear. Approved footwear should be soccer type shoes with bars or cleats made out of nylon, rubber, or leather. And referee's do inspect the shoes before a game starts. The shin guards should be made of rubber or plastic, and they must entirely covered by the stockings when worn. The jersey, and shorts, of each player on the team should be the same color. All jerseys must have a number permanently attached to it. The size is up to the league. If both teams have the same color uniforms, the home team must have a pullover shirt of a different color, to put on over their numbered jersey.

Players may ***not*** wear a cast, splints, jewelry (even if covered with tape), metal spikes, or detachable spikes. They can wear religious or medical

BALL SIZE vs AGE GROUPS			
AGE GROUPS OR DIV. "CYC"	BALL SIZE	CIRCUMFERENCE (INCHES)	WEIGHT (OUNCES)
All Divisions		27 - 28	14 - 16
"AYSO"			
U6	3	23 - 25	10 -12
U8	3	23 - 25	10 -12
U10	4	25 - 26	12 -14
U12	4	25 - 26	12 -14
U14	5	26.5 - 28	14 - 16

FIGURE 119

medallions, but they must be taped to the body under the uniform. Sometimes gloves, soft caps without a brim, and track suit pants, can be worn with the referee's permission. The goalkeepers wear colors that will distinguish them from the players and the referee. Sometimes it's the whole uniform, and sometimes just a pullover shirt or vest. *SEE FIGURE 120* for some typical equipment used in game.

Other Equipment

One of the most important pieces of equipment required during the game, is a ball. Soccer balls do vary in size and color *(SEE PAGE 132)*. The chart will give you the size of ball your son or daughter should be practicing with *(SEE FIGURE 119)*. Balls are inflated with air. If the ball burst during the game, the

SHORTS   JERSEY   PULLOVER VESTS

GOALKEEPER SHIRT   SHIN GUARDS   STOCKINGS   GLOVES

HEADER HEADBAND   SHOES   BALL

FIGURE 120
Typical on field Equipment

game is immediately stopped and the ball is replaced. Balls must also be of regulation weight, when inflated from 8.5 lbs/sq inch up to 15.6 lbs/sq inch.

Other available equipment used mostly in soccer training are shooting targets, backyard goals, garage nets, kicking trainers, dribbling trainers, speed ladders, header trainers, and leg strength builders *(SEE FIGURE 121)*. Head

SHOOTING TARGETS

LEG STRENGTH BUILDER

SPEED LADDERS

GARAGE NET

CONE SETS

BACKYARD GOAL

TETHER KICK TRAINER

STARKICK KICKING TRAINER

DRIBBLING TRAINER

FIGURE 121
Some Typical Training
Equipment

bands and wrist bands are used to soak up sweat. The header head band is for head safety when practicing headers. Cone sets are used a lot to mark training courses and small fields.

Some of this equipment is available in sporting goods stores, and athletic equipment stores. Many of the training aids are available on the "InterNet". And believe it or not, many of them are not too expensive.

Try these other excellent books for teaching your Son or Daughter sports Fundamentals.

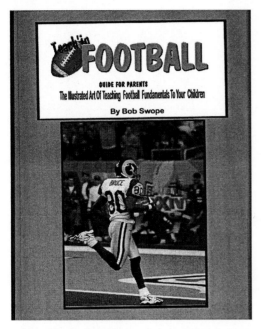

Teach'in Football - Teach your son all the basic fundamentals he needs, to play the game of football. Mom and dad, you will have fun teaching him, and he will have more fun playing the game because he will feel like he knows what he is doing. This book is complete with everything both of you need to know. It covers all the positions, new parent orientation to football, equipment required, field size, and game rules.
ISBN 0-9705827-4-9, soft cover paperback, 8 x 10-1/2, 138 pages.

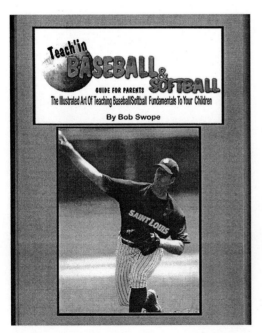

Teach'in Baseball & Softball - Teach your son or daughter all the basic fundamentals they need, to play the game of baseball or softball, and all in one book. Mom and dad, you will have fun teaching them, and they will have more fun playing the game because they will feel like they know what they are doing. This book is complete with everything both of you need to know. It covers all the positions, new parent orientation to the game, equipment required, field size, and game rules.
ISBN 0-9705827-2-2, soft cover paperback, 8 x 10-1/2, 161 pages.

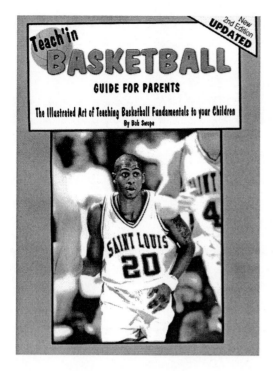

Teach'in Basketball - Teach your son or daughter all the basic fundamentals they need to play the game of basketball. Mom and dad, you will have fun teaching them, and they will have more fun playing the game because they will feel like they know what they are doing. This book is complete with everything both of you need to know. It covers all the positions, new parent orientation to the game, equipment required, court size, and game rules.
ISBN 0-9705827-6-5, 2nd edition updated, soft cover paperback, 8 x 10-1/2, 151 pages.

Teach'in Track & Field - Teach your son or daughter all the basic fundamentals they need to excell in track and field events. Mom and dad, you will have fun teaching them, and they will have more fun learning the events because they will feel like they know what they are doing. This book is complete with everything both of you need to know. It covers all the events, new parent orientation to track and field, equipment required, track size, and most basic rules.
ISBN 0-9705827-5-7, soft cover paperback, 8 x 10-1/2, 180 pages.

These books and other Jacobob Press Ltd. books are available from your local bookstore, just ask for them, or by calling the supplier at (314) 843-4829.

Index

A

Abs, strengthening.........................31
Agility Drills................................21
Athletic Equipment Stores.............151
Attitude Development.......................8
AYSO age groups.........................132

B

Backward Roll Drill.......................25
Ball sizes..................................148
Blocking, General.........................72

C

Center Backs, General...................13
Center Defenders, General..............13
Casts.......................................148
Catching, General.......................102
Chipping the Ball.........................88
Clearing the Ball........................121
Cone Sets.................................150
Controlled Falling Drills................24
Cool downs................................32
Coordination & Agility, Gen............21
Corner Kicks.........................98, 138
Crossover Foot Drill......................21
CYC Divisions............................132

D

Dead Ball Kicks...........................94
Defenders, General........................13
Defending, General......................119
Defense, One on One....................121
Defense, Zone...........................121
Defensive Game..........................127
   Defensive Team Members........128
   Defensive Scoring.................127
   What Defense Does................127
   What Defensive Players Do........128
Deflecting Shots, General...............106
Direct Free Kick.....................94, 138
Distributing the Ball, General...........109
Dribbling, General........................32
Drills & Exercises, Gen..................16

Drills For Ball Control (Juggling).........50
   Side to Side with the Feet.................53
   Topping with the Feet......................52
   Using the Feet 51
   With the Chest............................54
   With the Head 55
   With the Thigh 55
Drills For Blocking/Stealing 72
Drills for Chipping & Volleying 88
   Chipping 88
   Full Volley Kick 89
   Half Volley Kick.........................91
Drills For Controlled Falling 24
   Backward Roll 25
   Forward Roll 24
   Over the Rolling Body 27
   Over the Top Jumping 26
   Shoulder Roll 25
Drills for Coordin'tn/Agility 21
   Crossover Foot..........................21
   Monkey Walk 23
   Running Backwards 22
Drills for Defending & Marking.........119
   Defending, General.....................119
   Ball & Cover...........................120
   Clearing................................121
   Marking................................121
Drills for Dribbling 32
   Heel of Foot 36
   Inside of Foot 33
   Instep of Foot 36
   Outside of Foot 34
   Sole of the Foot 37
Drills for Faking/Tricking 73
   The Head & Eyes 75
   Quick Feet Direction Change..........77
   The Cruyff Turn.....................80 The
   Drag Back Turn.....................79
   The Locomotive (Leo) 74
   The Maradona Move...................78
   The Slow & Go 73
Drills for Goalkeeping 101
   Belt/Chest High Catches 102
   Building a Wall Defense 114

Defensive Techniques 111
Deflecting Shots 106
Deflecting with the Palm 108
Distributing the Ball 109
Diving Catches 105
Goal Kicks 111
Low Catches 103
Over the Head Catches...................104
Position Around Goal 111
Punching the Ball 107
Ready Position 100
Stopping Dribbling Forwards 114
Stopping Penalty Kicks...............113
Drills for Heading 64
Drills for Kicking & Shooting Goals.....91
Corner Kick 98
Direct Free Kick 96
Indirect Free Kick 94
Off a Crossing Pass 93
Penalty Kick...............................100
Straight On or Angle 92
Drills for the Kickoff 116
Defensive Techniques/Tactics........118
Offensive Techniques/Tactics 117
Drills for Passing...........................38
Drop Pass 44
Give and Go Pass 49
Hip Turn Pass 45
Inside part of Foot 41
Outside of Foot 43
Outside/Inside Instep 41
Over the Head (Bicycle) 46
Overlap Run Pass 48
Straight Ahead Instep 40
Drills for Protecting Ball 82
Shielding the Ball 82
Drills for Running/Quick/Endurance ..83
Endurance 87
Quickness Speed Bursts 86
Running Laps 84
Wind Sprints 84
Wind Sprint Ladders 85
Drills for Strength 27
Dumbbell Pullover 31

Knee Bend Pulls 30
Leg Lifts 28
Half Squats 29
Sit Up Crunches 28
Wall Sits 29
Transverse Ab Strengthening 31
Drills for Throwing 60
Goalkeeper 61
Side Line Throw In 63
Drills for Tackling 64
The Ground 65
The Head On 66
The Hook 71
The Shoulder 68
The Side 67
The Slide 69
Drills for Trapping/Receiving 56
Using the Feet 56
With the Chest/Body 58
With the Head 60
With the Thighs 59
Drop Balls................................125
Dual Officiating system...................135
Dumbbells Pullover Drill..................31
E
Endurance, General..........................83
Ephedra (Warning)..........................10
Equipment, General.......................147
Equipment, Miscellaneous.......149, 150
Equipment, Training.......................150
Equipment, Typ.on field..................149
Exercises Warm Up/Stretching...............16
F
Faking, General..............................73
Field Presence Drills......................24
Forward, General..........................12
Formations............................123
Forward Roll Drill........................24
Fouls.....................................138
Fullback, General.......................13
Fundamentals.................11
Defenders, Stoppers, Fullbacks.........13
Forwards/Strikers/Wingbacks........12
Goalkeeper 15

Midfielders/Left/Right....................13
Sweeper 14
What are they............................11

G
Game of Soccer............................124
Game Rules, General............................131
Gloves............................149
Goal Kick............................111, 134
Goalkeeper, General............................15
Goalkeeping, General............................101

H
Half Squats Drill............................29
Hamstring Stretch............................18
Head Coach............................9
Headbands............................150, 151
Header Headband............................149, 150
Heading, General............................64
Health Habits............................10
Hustle............................10

I
Improving............................8
Indirect Free Kick............................96, 139
Influence, Parental............................8
InterNet Shopping............................151
Introduction............................6

J
Jersey's............................148, 149
Jewelry............................148
Juggling, General............................50
Judges............................134

K
Kicking, General............................91
Kicks, Free............................94-97
Kickoff 's............................116, 132
Knee Bend Pulls............................30
Knockout Competition............................133

L
Leg Lifts............................28

M
Marking............................121
Medals 148
Medallions, medical or religious.....148
Midfielders, General............................13

Misconduct............................137
Monkey Walk............................23
N
New Parent Orientation 124
O
Offensive Game............................125
How goals are Scored............................125
Offensive Scoring............................125
Offensive Team Members............................126
What Offensive Players Do............................126
What Offense does............................126
Officials............................134
Where are they located............................137
Who are the Officials............................135
Why have Officials............................134
Offsides............................140, 141
One on One Defense............................121
Organize your Teaching............................15
Orientation, New Parents............................124
Over the Rolling Body Drill............................27
Over the Top Jumping Drill............................26
Overtime Games............................133
P
Passing, General............................38
Penalty Kicks............................100, 139
Penalty Shootout............................133
Penalties............................138-141
Playing Field, Regular............................129
Playing Field, Short Sided............................130
Protecting the Ball............................82
Q
Quickness, General............................83
R
Receiving, General............................56
Red Card............................140
Referee's............................134
Assistant Referee's............................135-137
Assistant Referee's Signals............................137
Referee's Signals............................136
Respect............................10
Running Backwards Drill............................22
Running, General............................83
Rules............................131-134

S

Safety, General...........................147
Shin Guards........................ 148, 149
Shirts.....................................148, 149
Shoes...............................83, 148-149
Shorts...................................149, 149
Shoulder Roll Drill...........................25
Signals, Asst Referee..............137
Signals, Referee.......................136
Sit Ups Drill..............................28
Socks....................................148, 149
Soccer, Game of..........................124
Soccer Terminology.....................141
Speed, General...........................83
Splints...............................148
Stealing, General...........................72
Stockings (socks)....................148, 149
Stoppers, (Center Defenders) Gen.......13
Strength, General..........................27
Stretching...................................16
Strikers, General..........................12
Substitutions...............................133
Sudden (death) procedure.....................133
Sweeper, General...........................14

T

Tackling, General..............................64
Teaching, Organize your......................15
Team Members.........................126-128
Terminology, Soccer.......................141
Throw Ins................................63, 134
Throwing, General...........................60
Time Interval (For game)....................131
Training Equipment........................150
Trapping, General..........................56
Tricking, General..........................73

U

Uniform....................................148, 149

V

Vest, Pull over..............................149
Volleying, General.......................88

W

Walls, Defensive.........................114
Wall Sits Drill...........................29

Warm Up/Stretching Exercises.........16
Abductors Stretch 19
Active Hip Stretch 18
Ankle Stretch...........................21
Calf Stretch...................... 20
Hip Extensor Stretch 19
Hip Stretch...........................17
Jogging 16
Knee to Chest Stretch 20
Overhead Stretch 17
Seated Pelvic Stretch.................... 17
Seated Straddle Groin...................18
Warnings 6
Wingbacks, General.........................13
Wrist bands...........................151

Y

Yellow Card..................................139
Youth Soccer Teams........................132

Z

Zone Defense.............................121